Contents

3

The Beginnings Of Hinduism

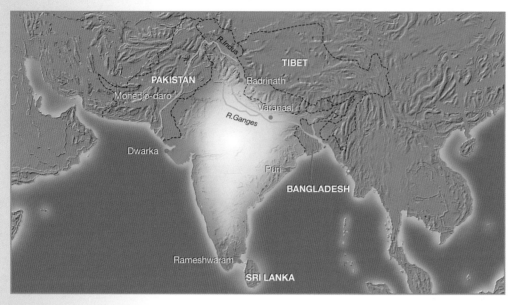

◄ *The land where Hinduism developed. Find the River Indus. The orange-shaded areas show where most Hindus live now*

Hinduism is older than any other living religion. Hindus believe that it has always existed and always will exist. This book will use the word Hinduism, but Hindus themselves usually call it Sanatana Dharma. It means the **Eternal** Law.

The word Hindu comes from the River Indus. It was first used by the Persians. In the beginning it described the region and the people who lived there and not just their religion.

Hinduism developed gradually as different groups of people met and shared their ideas and their ways of practising their beliefs. Some **rituals** and ideas stayed the same, while others died out. Some got mixed up together and became new ones.

India is an enormous country, over fourteen times the size of Britain. The northern part is close to the Himalayas, a *land of snow*. The south is near the **Equator**, very warm all the year round.

People in different areas live in different ways. They have different languages and ways of dressing. So, as Hinduism slowly spread from the north to the south, it developed in different ways in different parts of the country. But most people came to share the same basic beliefs.

Hinduism has developed its beliefs and ceremonies over thousands of years. New ideas have been introduced and placed alongside old ones.

It is a rich, fertile religion that is like a luxurious growth, with many branches, leaves and flowers.

It can be confusing to outsiders, with its many rituals, symbols, stories and scriptures. Many non-Hindus ask questions about the holy statues of many gods and goddesses. Hindus appear to worship more than one God; though some do, many do not. There are varieties of belief.

- Some Hindus are polytheists, worshipping many **deities**.
- Some Hindus treat all the deities as aspects of one God.
- Others see only some deities as aspects of one God, with others being lesser divine beings, or holy souls, rather like the angels and saints in Christianity.

As some of the earliest Scriptures state:

> - God is One, but wise men call Him by different names.
>
> *Rig Veda 1.164.46*

To many Hindus, the various gods and goddesses represent different forms and aspects of the one God.

There were people living near the River Indus about five thousand years ago. They built large cities. One of these was called Mohenjo-daro. **Archaeologists** have dug up this city and discovered many things about the Indus people and their civilisation.

They found that the ancient people here had brick houses and paved streets. There was running water and a drainage system. It was an advanced civilisation for its time. (People in Britain were living in simple villages and huts at this time.)

There were female statues which looked like mother goddesses in Mohenjo-daro. They often had smoke stains on them, as if there had been a lamp burning in front of them.

Dead people were buried. Often they were given food and drink to take with them on their journey to the next life. The bowls and cups sometimes had pictures of animals, and gods and goddesses on them.

The Aryans came to the River Indus from Central Asia about 3,500 years ago. Their name means 'noble people'. They worshipped round a fire, on which they made **sacrifices**, including animals. There were three main reasons for this:

- It showed that they were sorry for doing wrong, and **pardoned** their sins.
- It formed a link between them and their **ancestors**.

- It persuaded the gods to make them healthy and rich, and give them lots of children and cattle.

Aryan gods were connected with the sky and everything to do with the sky, like the sun and the wind. Gods were more important than goddesses.

At first the Aryans fought the Indus people. They believed that Indra, god of thunder, helped them in battle. This is how one of their holy books describes him.

- Without whom men do not conquer, whom when fighting they call on for help; who has been a match for everyone, who moves the immovable: he, O man, is Indra.

But sometimes groups of Aryans made friends with the local people and joined with them to attack other groups. Others began to live near to each other in peace. They found out about each other's religions and way of life. They traded with each other and **intermarried**.

Aryans settled down and built large cities, mainly along the River Ganges in Northern India. Some of their ideas began to change as they mixed with the local people. For example, they began to feel it was wrong to kill animals to offer to the gods.

5

A **residential** area of Mohenjo-daro ▶

The archaeological remains at Mohenjo-daro show how modern Hindus still draw some of their practices from their ancient heritage – ritual bathing, and praying before the sacred fire.

Most religions use water and fire in their worship, in different ways – candles, lamps, washing before prayer, or sprinkling with holy water. Deep truths and feelings are symbolised by these elements.

Water is cleansing, fresh, and gives life.

Fire burns bright, suggesting the light of truth, and the power of God.

▲ Hindus today carry out many ceremonies in front of a holy fire

1 Copy this paragraph into your book, choosing the correct words from the brackets.

Sanatana Dharma means (Endless Story; Eternal Law). The Indus people lived near the River (Inn; Indus). Aryan means (noble, noisy). Hinduism developed in modern-day (America; India). It contains the ideas of (one group; many groups) of people.

2 On a clean page, copy the map on page 4. Use your atlas to find the modern names of the orange-shaded countries. Write them on your map and colour those countries in orange.

3 a) Give three reasons why the Aryans worshipped their gods.

b) For each, say whether or not you think it is a good reason. Explain your answers.

c) Write your own description of the god Indra.

d) Write down three words which you think describe the way the Aryans felt about Indra. Give your reason for each.

4 a) What has been discovered about the use of fire and water in ancient Aryan religion at Mohenjo-daro?

b) How do modern Hindus use water and fire?

c) Talk about a time when you have had a swim in cool water, or quenched your thirst in the heat.

d) Light a candle in front of the class and stare at this for a minute. What ideas and feelings come to mind?

e) Why do you think fire and water are used as symbols of God?

New ideas and insights slowly developed from Hinduism's ancient beginnings. The next major development was with the teachings of holy men, monks who gave up all wealth and attachments to others. They prayed and **meditated** for long hours in the forests, often in groups, supporting and encouraging each other. Then they taught disciples. A Hindu teacher is called a guru. This development lasted from about the seventh century BCE to the fifth century BCE.

The holy men meditated on what was true and what was false, the nature of life, the universe, and God. What they came to realise was written down in a series of questions and answers.

The Aum syllable is used in meditation. The Sanskrit letters are the equivalent of 'A', 'U' and 'M'. It is the sound which represents God. Some say this is the vibration of life, the energy by which the universe was created. The holy men spoke of one life force, or spirit, behind all things. This is Brahman. The word comes from Sanskrit 'brh' meaning 'growth'.

▲ *The Aum syllable*

- The whole universe is Brahman.
- The womb and origin of all that comes into being.
- From Him springs forth the breath of life.

One teacher used a visual aid to explain where Brahman was.

The holy men sometimes spoke of Brahman as personal, and sometimes as impersonal, more like a spiritual force. Some Hindus teach that God is personal, and some say God is abstract and impersonal. There are different traditions. Some Hindus believe that the impersonal aspect of God is the highest, and see all the personal deities as ways of helping people worship something they do not understand – it is hard to worship a force! They are steps along the way, and illusions, really, until people are ready to understand God as a force.

Others see the personal nature of God as the most sublime aspect. God is *really* personal, and things like loving relationships are therefore the most real things in the universe.

Joyful praise to a personal God is called Bhakti yoga. **Yoga** means 'way' or 'unity', and there are many different types of yoga that can be used to find God. The holy men in the forests developed exercises to help them meditate (the type of yoga practised in the West is Hatha yoga, a basic set of physical exercises that can be developed into meditation techniques). Another type of yoga involves doing good deeds. Hinduism has many paths that can lead to God.

Hinduism therefore allows people to be aware of God as vast and mysterious, but also as personal and loving.

8

▲ *A Hindu father embracing his child outside the shrine in the temple*

▲ *Endless, infinite space . . . vast distances and silent mystery*

1 What did the holy men mean by 'Brahman'?
2 Copy the Aum syllable and explain what this means and how it is used.
3 What was the holy man trying to teach the child with the bowl of water and salt?
4 Explain what Bhakti yoga is. Why is this type of yoga important for some Hindus?
5 Look at the photos of outer space, and a parent. What ideas and feelings do these give you? What do they suggest about God?
6 Design your own symbol for God. What do you want it to say? Will it suggest vastness and greatness, mystery or something loving that you can trust and is safe?
7 Think of a word or phrase that would be calming and peaceful to say over and over again, as Hindus chant 'Aum'. What might this be? Draw this on a full page, and design it to look special and colourful.

We have seen how many centuries ago there was an advanced civilisation in parts of India. Hindu culture never lost the art of learning new ideas, and their merchants travelled around the known world, trading goods and sharing knowledge. Hindus invented two games that are still enjoyed in Europe – snakes and ladders and chess. Snakes and ladders is a game of ups and downs, just like life. While your moves up and down on the board depend upon the chance throw of a dice, Hindus believe that what happens to us in life is not by accident, but we bring it upon ourselves by our past actions.

Hindus teach that there is such a thing as karma. This can be called fate or destiny, but not in a Western sense. A Hindu believes that destiny can be changed by our actions. Karma is the law of action and reaction that applies to all living beings. Good actions earn good karma, whereas bad actions bring evil results. It is like throwing a rock into a pool – ripples circle out all over the surface. What we do has an impact, sometimes long after the event. Whatever we do to others, either good or bad, will come back to us.

We can easily understand how different actions bring different results, for example, one person shares, and this makes people trust them, like them, or speak well of them in the future. The other is sly and steals. They will get a bad reputation and people will not trust them. Our actions bring their own judgement upon us.

What we do has an impact long after our initial actions, like ripples on a pond.

▲ Snakes and ladders is a game of ups and downs. It is just like life. The Hindus invented it. Chess also comes from ancient India

▲ Our actions affect our lives, and those around us

The Hindus of the fourth and fifth centuries CE made important contributions to science. Astronomers knew that the Earth was round and that it turned on its **axis**. Some of the ancient Greeks had suspected this, too, but people in the Western world did not accept this until over one thousand years later. Christopher Columbus made his journey across the ocean to find an alternative route to India, and he discovered America in 1492. He took this route because he believed, with some others, that the world was actually round.

Mathematicians developed two ideas which changed the way numbers were used. One was the idea and the symbol for zero. The other was the system of what are called Arabic numbers (1, 2, 3 etc). The system was later introduced into the West by Arabs. But they got the idea from Hindu mathematicians.

▲ *Many of our ideas depend upon knowledge from ancient India*

▲ *Ways of producing fine textiles were developed in India*

Men working in industry developed ways of producing fine **textiles**. Cotton, calico, chintz and cashmere are all fabrics named after places in India. Arabs and Europeans learned the **techniques** from the Hindus.

1 What ideas did Hindus have in the past that the Western world has benefited from?
2 Design a Karma game. Unlike 'Snakes and Ladders', this does not depend upon blind chance. Have different actions, which result in going up/down, backwards/forwards, depending on whether they are good or bad.

There are many holy books in the Hindu religion. These are called Shastras (scriptures). The most important Shastras are the Vedas. These are the oldest holy books in the world. The word *veda* means knowledge. Hindus believe the Vedas came from God and contain everything to be known about the world.

The Vedas include hymns for the priests to sing, prayers, and instructions on how to live and worship. At the end of each Veda are sections dealing with the real meaning of life and the universe.

These sections are called the Upanishads. They are mainly questions and answers. It is as if students are questioning their teachers so they can find out about the ideas of Hinduism.

At first holy men and teachers learned the Vedas by heart. But the Aryans wrote them down over three thousand years ago. They were written as poems in Sanskrit, the Aryan language.

> ● Sanskrit is a very complicated language. I did a degree in Sanskrit, but when our priest speaks Sanskrit I can't understand it! So he speaks Sanskrit in the temple and then he explains it in **Hindi** and English.

The Upanishads contain many of the ideas of the holy men who meditated in the forests, and who spoke of God as Brahman. They sought a way for the soul to be unified with God, and to escape the material world.

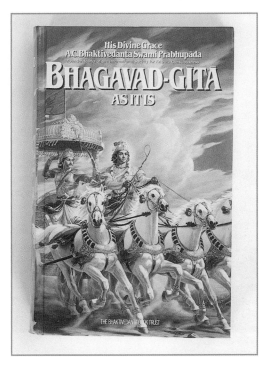

▲ English translation of the Bhagavad Gita

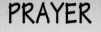

PRAYER

ASATO MAA SAD GAMAYAA
TAMASO MA AJYOTIR GAMAYAA
MRITYORMA AMRITAM GAMAYAA

O God, lead us from untruth to truth, Lead us from darkness to light, and lead us from death to immortality.

▲ A Sanskrit prayer, with English translation

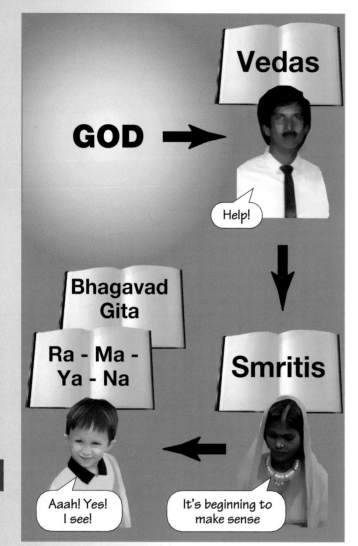

▲ *The Hindu holy books*

The stories are about the various Hindu deities, kings, heroes and other famous people. They give examples of the best way to live. This Hindu woman explains what happens in her Temple.

● Since I've been here, I haven't heard anybody reading the Vedas. Mostly the priest teaches about Bhagavad Gita and **Ramayana**. He reads Sanskrit first and then he explains in Hindi.

The Mahabharata and Ramayana are two long poems about the adventures of ancient heroes, many of whom are seen as divine. The Gita is part of the Mahabharata. There are also the Puranas, popular tales about the deities and their appearances on Earth. The most popular is the Bhagavad Purana, especially the tenth book which tells about the life of Krishna.

The Vedas are in four collections, and the Rig Veda is probably the most popular, with its many hymns in praise of the deities. The Vedas also contain a great deal of knowledge about science, mathematics and medicine, which was very advanced for its time.

'Upanishad' means 'to sit at the feet' and this meant that disciples went out to learn from holy men in the forests. There are thirteen main Upanishads.

The Vedas are not easy for most people to understand. So Hindu teachers wrote the **Smritis** to try to explain them. The most important Smritis were written about 2,500 years ago.

Even the Smritis are quite difficult to follow. So there are many more books, in simpler language. They help Hindus to understand their religion through stories.

▲ *Lord Krishna*

The Mahabharata is the 'great history of ancient India'. It is about a battle between the forces of good and evil. It is based upon a struggle for the throne, and the threat to the lives of five princes.

> The eldest brother of the Kurus was blind, and so he could not become king. His brother, Pandu, became king, instead.

> Pandu wanted to live as a holy man, and so he gave the kingdom to his brother, Dhritarashtra.

> The king took Pandu's five sons into his palace and treated them as his own. His own sons were jealous, and planned to kill them. They escaped to the forest, led by Prince Arjuna.

> The blind king heard of this, and returned half the stolen kingdom to the Pandavas (sons of Pandu). The Kurus even cheated them out of this. A great battle started that lasted for eighteen days. Eventually, the Pandavas won and ruled wisely.

▲ The story of the Mahabharata

The Bhagavad Gita or Song of the Lord is a very popular part of a longer poem. It tells the story of how two groups of cousins go to war to decide who should be the next king. On the battlefield, Prince Arjuna does not want to fight his own relations. In his dilemma, he is overcome by grief and confusion. He turns for advice to Krishna who is acting as his chauffeur. Lord Krishna instructs Arjuna for nearly an hour.

Finally Krishna convinces Arjuna that it is his duty to fight. He tells Arjuna that only the soldiers' bodies will die. Nobody can destroy their souls. So Arjuna's army fights and wins the battle.

The Gita sums up the main beliefs of Hinduism. Its message is that you will only be satisfied with your life if you do your duty with an attitude of loving service to God. For many Hindus, it is their favourite holy book. The Hindu leader Mahatma Gandhi wrote:

- When doubts haunt me, when disappointments stare me in the face, and when I see not one ray of light on the horizon, I turn to the Bhagavad Gita and find a verse to comfort me. I immediately begin to smile in the midst of **overwhelming** sorrow.

   My life has been full of tragedies. If they have not left any visible effect on me, I owe it to the teaching of the Bhagavad Gita.

▼ Krishna teaches Arjuna and reveals himself as God

Prince Arjuna faced members of his family in battle. He did not want to fight them, but they had done wrong and cheated many people.

I have no heart for this... my own kinsmen face me...

You know it is your duty to punish wrongdoing, and to restore justice.

Krishna explained that only the bodies of the soldiers could be killed. Their souls would live on, and be reborn.

Whichever way you choose eventually leads to me... The highest is bhakti, for I give my very self to those who worship me with love.

Krishna explained that there are many ways to God, such as meditation, good works, and also loving service, bhakti.

Krishna revealed his glory to Arjuna, as an appearance of God on Earth.

1 **a)** Unscramble these letters to find Hindu holy books.
   DASHAINSUP; SISTRIM;
   DASEV; HAVADAGB AGTI.

   b) Write a sentence about each to explain what it is.

   c) For each one, say why it is important to Hindus.

2 **a)** Tell the story of Arjuna in pictures.

   b) What can you learn from this story?

   c) Do you think hearing stories is a good way to learn about how you should behave? Give your reasons.

3 Make up a story about a struggle between good and evil. This can be set in the past, today, or in the future. Design a cover for it, and conclude it with a moral, and with two or three wise sayings about how we should live our lives.

4 **a)** Read what Mahatma Gandhi wrote about the Gita. What effect did reading it have on him?

   b) Write about a time when something has cheered you up.

Each Hindu does not have to believe exactly the same things as every other Hindu. Each expects that others will have some different beliefs. It will depend on their background, their education or what they have worked out for themselves. But there are some beliefs which nearly all Hindus accept.

There is one God behind the many shapes and forms around us. God might be called by different names, usually Vishnu, Shiva or Krishna – words meaning 'protecting' or 'auspicious' or 'all-attractive'. God is everywhere, in everything and eternal. But we cannot see God with our present eyes, or hear him with our material ears. God is spiritual. This is what Mahatma Gandhi wrote about God.

- Whilst everything around me is ever changing, ever dying, there is underlying all that change a living power that is changeless, that holds all together, that creates, dissolves and recreates. That power or spirit is God.

And this is how Brahman is described in the Upanishads.

- You are woman. You are man.
  You are the dark-blue bee
  and the green parrot with the red eyes.
  The lightning is your child.
  You are the seasons of the year
  and the sea.
  You are part of everything.
  You are everywhere.
  Everywhere that is, is born of you.

The part of Brahman which is in people, and in all living things, is called the Atman, the eternal soul. Deep down, we are all really a part of God. Here are two explanations of this idea.

- The soul is the real you. The body is like a car that you're driving for this particular life.

- The body is just like a bag. It's a bag full of blood and bones and organs. It's not as important as the soul.

When the body dies, the soul moves to live in another body. This change is called samsara or reincarnation. It happens many times. But we do not usually remember our other lives.

▲ *The Namaste greeting*

Hindus greet each other with 'Namaste', meaning 'I bow to you in respect'. Something of God lives in everyone.

The Upanishads declare 'Tat tvam asi' or 'You are That'. Each soul is a tiny part of God, who is great. We are the soul within. That is why Hindus bow and join their hands in respect when meeting someone. They bow to the Atman within.

One of the Upanishads explains why love must be shown to all living things:

- A wife loves her husband not for his own sake . . . but because the Atman lives in him . . . Children are loved not for their own sake, but because the Atman lives in them . . .

There are many layers to what makes up a person – feelings, thoughts and conscience, for example. What is the conscience? Hindus believe that this is the part of us that hears and responds to God. Deep at the centre of our lives, the deepest layer, is God, who dwells in all living things.

Think of this as two birds in a tree: one is smaller, eating berries; the other is larger. Each individual person is one, and God is a friend, a companion bird who is greater. The body is like the tree, and we are like the bird eating the fruits. This is aware of a greater presence, of God as all around, filling the universe. Each soul perceives God through the conscience and our intelligence.

Or, think of a light bulb lighting up a room. The sunlight shines in, too, when the sun comes up, and is greater and stronger than the little light.

As we go through life the body changes and grows. We think differently as a teenager, than as a young child and even differently as an adult. But who is the real person within? What changes and what stays the same?

In a way, we are always different, always changing. In another way, we are the same person within, doing the changing. Think of a parable:

- A man once lent his friend £20. The friend moved away, and the years passed. They lost touch with each other. One day, they met in a crowd. Though it had been so long, they thought they recognised each other. They looked carefully at each other and then they talked. The man remembered the £20.
  'What do you mean?' asked his friend, 'I'm not the same person as I was then. I'm different!'
  Would the man have been impressed by this?

We can point to different parts of our bodies. But can we point to ourselves?

▲ *Three generations of a Hindu family in South London. What different outlook on life will each generation have?*

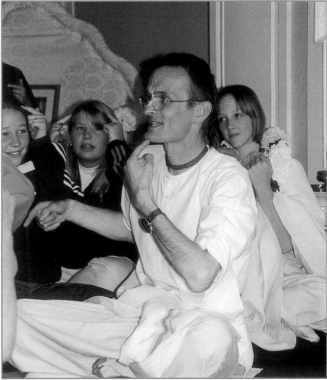

▲ *Can you point to yourself?*

1 a) On a piece of paper, draw an outline of a body and label this 'Atman'. Inside the body, draw anything that is personal or special to your life, the things which make you 'you'.

b) 'You are more than just your physical body.' Discuss this in class.

c) Try this game: point to your head; point to your left hand; point to your ear; point to your knees; point to your elbow; point to yourself. What did you do for the last command?

d) Hindus see the individual atman as a part of God, like a raindrop and the ocean. Think of some other comparisons to explain the relationship of the soul to God.

e) Think of some other examples of the relationship of the soul to God, the self to the Self, like the birds in the tree.

Everything we do makes something else happen. And everything that happened in our soul's previous lives makes things happen in the next life. This link between actions is called the law of karma. You earn good or bad karma for everything you do.

If you have lived a good life, the soul will be born as a person who is more important or happier. If your life has not been so good, the soul will be born as a more unlucky person. It may even be as an animal, tree or plant.

But the soul always has the chance to improve. Then it will be born into a better life next time round. This is how one of the Upanishads describes it.

● Those whose conduct here has been good will quickly **attain** a good birth. But those whose conduct here has been evil will quickly attain an evil birth – birth as a dog, or birth as a pig.

A person makes for himself his next life as a result of his hopes, actions, failures, disappointments and achievements performed during this present life. A caterpillar, before it leaves one leaf, makes sure that his front feet have been firmly fixed on the next leaf. So a soul creates its next life even before it departs from the present one.

People have a duty, called Dharma, to do what is right and just. We know this in our conscience, and through the Scriptures. Dharma is also used to describe a Hindu's religion, the Eternal Law or Truth.

Another Hindu teaching is Ahimsa, non-violence. This means that people should not do anything to hurt other living beings.

Dharma and ahimsa can sometimes seem to clash. Some Hindus believe that it is right to fight in a just cause, just as Krishna advised Arjuna. Others take a vow that they will never use violence. This does not mean that they ignore their duty. Gandhi was a brave leader in the 1930s and 1940s who spoke out, held peace marches and demonstrations, and he was beaten and imprisoned, though he taught his followers to practise ahimsa.

▲ *A peaceful protest in Mumbai*

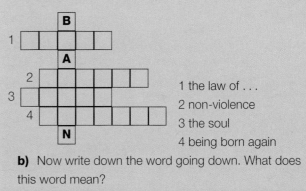

1 a) Draw this grid in your book and fill it in using the clues below.

1 the law of . . .
2 non-violence
3 the soul
4 being born again

b) Now write down the word going down. What does this word mean?

Hindus show respect to all nature. They should have a strong concern for the environment as they believe:

- we should be grateful for the gifts of God given through nature.
- all living beings have the soul within them.
- we have a responsibility to look after what God gives us.
- we should only accept those things granted to us and not steal that which belongs to another.

Hinduism sees the Earth as our mother. We all depend upon the planet, and food grows upon it. One old wise saying states, 'The Earth is our mother, and we are all her children.' Motherhood is very important in Hinduism, whether the Earth, a mother at the centre of the family, or cows and goddesses.

Hindus show special respect to the cow as a sacred animal. Krishna devotees in England look after cows in a special sanctuary. One devotee, Indriyesha Das, says, 'After a busy day, I love to relax and unwind by stroking and feeding the cows.'

If nature is filled with God, then forests and flowering trees are seen as sacred. Worship and offerings may be made at these places. The Mahabharata says, 'even if there is only one tree full of flowers and fruits in a village, that place becomes worthy of worship and respect.'

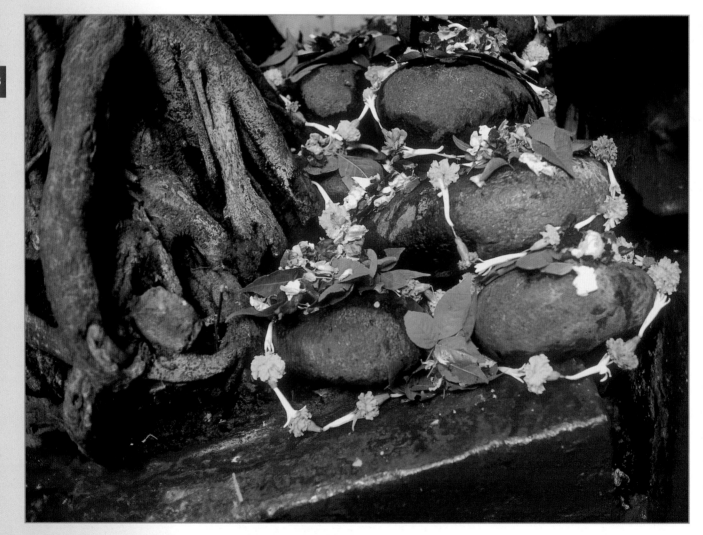

▲ *A tree offering in Calcutta*

The cow provides milk

This gives butter, ghee, yogurt, cream and cheese

Ghee is used for offerings

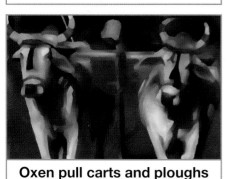

Oxen pull carts and ploughs

They are also used for milling and irrigation

Dried dung is used for walls, floors and for fuel and fertiliser

▲ *The cow is sacred and special to Hindus for all of the above reasons*

Cows are sacred because they provide so much for humans in rural India, and are seen as 'mothers'. The **sages** of ancient times tried to protect them, and, in time, they were seen as holy, as a gift from God.

Hindus are encouraged to be vegetarian, but this is only expected of priests, **sadhus**, and certain devotees, such as members of the International Society for Krishna Consciousness. Killing a living thing is seen to bring bad karma upon you. Even killing a plant can bring some bad karma, but by offering vegetarian food to God, this is cancelled.

Hindus prepare meals and offer some on a plate to a sacred image of a god in their home before they share this out. This is in thanksgiving for their meals, and forms an essential part of Hindu worship.

▲ *Offering food at a home shrine in England*

---

1 a) Talk in groups about situations where you think it would be right to fight.

b) Might there be situations where fighting would make things worse? What alternatives might there be?

c) Gandhi refused to fight, but he still did his duty, his dharma. How?

2 a) Draw a leaf or a tree and on each stem or branch write reasons why Hindus should respect the environment.

b) Write a poem about the Earth as our mother.

c) Work out a ceremony for either planting a new tree or encouraging people to respect a very old tree.

3 a) List the many things that cows can provide humans with.

b) Why do Hindus see the cow as sacred?

c) Why are many Hindus vegetarian?

Caste and Dharma

If you had to divide your class into sets, how would you do it? Maybe you would divide everyone according to how much pocket money they get. Or you might have twelve sets, grouping together people with the same birthday month.

If you grouped by amounts of pocket money, people would probably be in a different set if you asked them again the following year. But if you chose the second way, each person would always belong to the same set.

Hindus believe that people are divided into sets called varnas or classes. Some believe that each person belongs to the same varna for their whole life. Some think birth decides your varna, others your skill and merits.

There are four varnas, and in each one there are hundreds of smaller groups called jati. These divide people according to their **traditional** jobs. At one time, a Hindu could only do a certain job if he or she belonged to a particular caste.

There was an important reason for the caste system. Hindus believe that everyone has a special duty. This duty is called dharma. It means holy law.

A Hindu's dharma depends partly on which caste he or she belongs to. Those with certain skills have a duty to use them.

The varna you are born into is thought to depend on your actions in previous lives i.e. your Karma. Here are the varnas in order of importance.

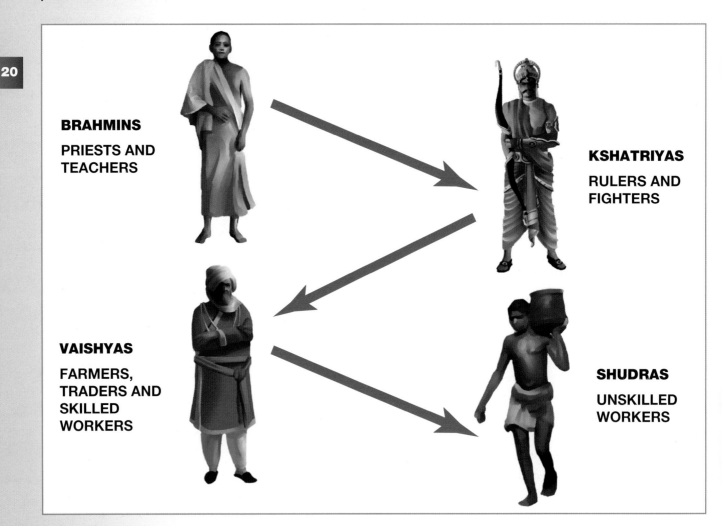

BRAHMINS

PRIESTS AND TEACHERS

KSHATRIYAS

RULERS AND FIGHTERS

VAISHYAS

FARMERS, TRADERS AND SKILLED WORKERS

SHUDRAS

UNSKILLED WORKERS

▲ The varnas in order of importance

There is also a fifth group of people. These do not belong to any class. They are sometimes called Untouchables. They do the really unpleasant jobs like cleaning the roads and toilets and getting rid of dead animals.

Until about fifty years ago Untouchables could not go into a high-caste temple, or into a house belonging to a Hindu in one of the three highest classes. They had to have their own wells. They could only travel by train if there was a special compartment for them. Today they are still among the poorest people in Hindu society.

Some Hindus will only mix closely with members of their own caste. They will only eat with people from the same caste. And they will not marry anyone from another caste.

▲ Untouchables do the unpleasant jobs

▲ Sometimes parents advertise for marriage partners for their children

Nowadays, it is illegal to **discriminate** against people because of their caste. But many Hindus still prefer to keep to their own caste, as this Hindu woman explains.

> ● Only people from our own caste can come here and eat with us off our plates. If we went out to eat it would only be with our own caste. There would never be any question of us eating with Untouchables. When we give food to our servant, he either eats off his own plate or we give him a clay plate which is then tossed away.

21

Historians debate how and why the caste system began. Many assume the Aryans made the earlier people of India into the two lower varnas, while they were the religious leaders and warriors. One of the old hymns in the Vedas declares that humans were made from one first man, and his many parts divided up into the varnas. The Brahmins were his mouth, his arms were the warriors, his thighs the farmers and traders, and his feet the craftsmen and workers. (Craftsmen who worked for someone else, and were not financially independent, belonged to the fourth varna.)

It is not clear how rigid this system was or what jobs people did until later on in Indian history. According to scholars, the laws of Manu were written between 200BCE and 200CE. These laid down long lists of rules for what type of work a caste member could do. Spiritual pollution was a key to this – the dirtier the job, the more polluting it was, and the higher castes could not work at these. The dirtiest jobs were for the Untouchables, and, to this day, leather workers tend to be from this group, as touching the skins of dead animals was forbidden to members of the four varnas.

There is a different tradition about the varnas in Hinduism, which might have been the oldest and purest. This rejects a rigid, hereditary system, and a person's varna is decided by their personality, their skills, their gifts, and their merits. This means that you can become a member of a different varna, if thought worthy, even though you are not born into it, by developing the right skills and attitudes. An old story tells of a youth who went to study with a holy man. When asked who his father was, he said he would have to go and ask his mother. His mother admitted that she did not know – she had been a society woman, living a wild life in her youth. He went back and told the holy man that he had no idea. The holy man stared at him and then said, 'I accept you as a Brahmin, for your soul is honest!'

The Gita gives this different idea of the four varnas. There, spiritual character and ability decide caste and not just birth:

▲ *Gandhi championed the rights of the Untouchables*

> ● Peacefulness, self-control, austerity, purity, tolerance, honesty, knowledge, wisdom and religiousness – they are the qualities by which the Brahmins work righteousness.
>
> *Gita 18:42*

This more creative, spiritual understanding of caste is not accepted by all, for some say that to have these qualities you must also be born in the right caste. The spiritual interpretation allows for Western converts to Hinduism, born out of the caste system, to become Hindu priests. This is true of those who have joined the International Society for Krishna Consciousness. They are accepted by most Hindus in India.

Untouchables are now referred to as 'dalits', 'the oppressed class', and many of them are the poorest in India. Gandhi campaigned for them, calling them 'the Children of God'. Some have gained an education and have risen to great things in Indian society, for example Ambedkar, who helped write the Indian Constitution in 1947.

Indian universities have actively encouraged lower castes to gain places in more recent years. An Indian President, K.R. Narayanan, was previously a dalit.

In modern India, the caste system still exerts great influence in the villages, where members of different jatis form guilds that help each other. It is breaking down in the towns, though, where many different jobs need to be done, and education is now more widely available. Most Temples are now open to all castes, but considerations of varna are most noticeable in marriage arrangements.

1 a) Discuss the advantages of following the same career as your parents.
   b) Imagine that you are being told that you have to do the same job as your parents, but you feel you have different skills and interests. Work out a role play in groups, where you have an argument and try to explain how you feel.

2 a) Name the different varnas.
   b) What were Hindus called who did not belong to a caste, and what are they called today?
   c) What kind of jobs did this lower group do, and why?
   d) What did Gandhi call this group? What point was he trying to make?

3 a) Why do people think the caste system began?
   b) How have things changed in modern day India?
   c) What does the Gita teach?
   d) Why can some Westerners become Hindu priests, even if they are not born in the Brahmin caste?

4 a) Think about groups in our own society. Are any disadvantaged through no fault of their own?
   b) Identify aspects of a class system in our own society.

◀ *These children struggle to learn an instrument*

Everyone faces challenges in life. If we aim to achieve something, we have a goal in mind. In football, we want to score and win; in archery, we aim at the target; in exams, we aim to study and pass. There are many goals like this as we go through life, but what do we really want to achieve in our lives? What are the most important things in life?

I want to be…   I want to do…

▲ *What is important in your life?*

In groups, design spider charts of all the goals that you have, all the big, special things you would like to achieve as you grow older. Then look at everyone's chart, and see if you can list the most important, special goals. Are these going to be easy to achieve?

Every Hindu has a goal. He or she has to work out the best way to reach it. The goal is for the soul to be free from samsara or being reborn. The goal is called Moksha, freedom, or release from constantly being reborn. You are free to be with God, like a raindrop returning to the ocean.

The way to reach this goal is to make sure that each rebirth takes the soul to a better kind of life. Think of it like climbing up a league table.

A bad life is a defeat – the soul is demoted. A good life stands for a win and promotion. Each promotion means that the soul will be able to understand a little more about the world and about God. Usually promotion means the soul is born as a person of a higher caste.

If you really try hard to obey your dharma, then you will go one step further up the league table. But the position you start at depends on the karma you have brought from your previous body.

● [This belief] explains why one character is good or bad or why one suffers and is miserable while another enjoys his life and is happy. We must not blame our parents. It is our own karma that results in joy or sorrow, pleasure or pain. Again and again man re-visits this earth to learn more lessons.

▲ *Fast cars and good food are nice, but they don't last for ever!*

We can have many goals in life and there are many things that we can enjoy, such as money, nice cars and good food. However, Hindus want to remind people that these things do not last for ever. The pleasures come to an end when the body dies. Spiritual things last for ever, and what really counts is being ready to join with God. This is to have riches beyond compare. A pure soul has a priceless treasure in his or her relationship with God. They are fully satisfied and do not need to be reborn. Rather they return to God in the spiritual world. This is Moksha. This is what two Hindu writers said about it.

- What I want to achieve – what I have been **striving** and **pining** to achieve these thirty years – is to see God face to face, to attain Moksha. All that I do by way of speaking and writing are directed to this same end.

- If you can rise above your karma, then the chances are you may not have to come back to this planet. You have the ability to go back to Heaven, to be with God. I'm not so attached to living as a human being forever on Earth, to be pulled in by [the **cycle** of] birth, death, disease, old age.

Here is a famous Hindu prayer from the Upanishads:

- Lead me from the unreal to the real;
  Lead me from darkness to light;
  Lead me from death to immortality.

1 a) Explain what Moksha is in a sentence.
b) What reason does each Hindu quoted in this chapter give for wanting to gain Moksha?
c) Look back at the charts of goals your class worked out. Which goals will die with the person, and which will live on, in some way?
d) Design a collage called 'Moksha', showing release from something lesser into something greater, or dark into light.

2 a) What do Hindus believe decides the kind of life we are born into?
b) In groups, discuss whether or not this is a good explanation for why some people may be born with a disability or very poor while others may be rich or healthy. Try to offer at least one other explanation.
c) Report the results of your group's discussion to the rest of your class.

Hindus have a choice of ways to lead them to Moksha. To some extent, a person can choose his or her own way, but all the ways work together. Good works, knowledge and love all go together. You cannot really have the one without the other.

These three paths are different forms of yoga, or ways to union with God.
- Karma – the way of action
- Jnana – the way of knowledge
- Bhakti – the way of loving service and devotion to God.

A fourth path, Raja, can be introduced too, which enables meditation and bodily control. Hatha yoga, so popular in the West as an exercise, is the first stage of this fourth path.

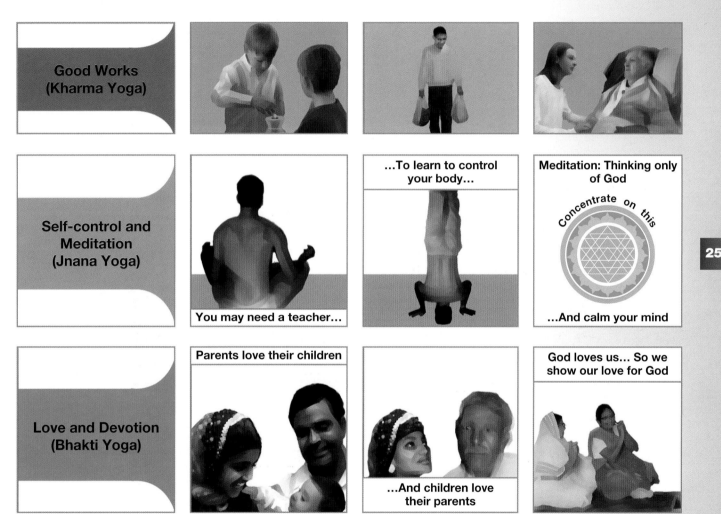

Good Works (Kharma Yoga)

Self-control and Meditation (Jnana Yoga)
You may need a teacher...
...To learn to control your body...
Meditation: Thinking only of God
Concentrate on this
...And calm your mind

Love and Devotion (Bhakti Yoga)
Parents love their children
...And children love their parents
God loves us... So we show our love for God

▲ *Ways to Moksha*

1 List the three paths to Moksha. What names are these given in the Sanskrit language?
2 Draw your own series of pictures to show Karma yoga in action.
3 Which of the three ways would you choose? Give reasons.
4 Can one of these paths be followed by ignoring the others? Explain.
5 Design three badges, one for each of the paths. Each one needs a symbol and the name of the path.
6 If you were to sit and meditate upon an object that was peaceful or suggested life or mystery to you, what might you choose? Write about this and draw it.

Hindus seem to worship many different gods. They have statues of different deities in their shrines and temples, and many stories about them in their Scriptures. Yet, Hinduism really teaches that there is one God only. There is a story of a child asking questions of her grandmother.

'How many gods are there?'

'Three thousand gods.'

The child asked again, 'How many gods are there?'

'Three hundred.'

Again, the child questioned, 'How many gods are there?'

'Three.'

One last time, the child quizzed the grandmother, 'How many gods are there?'

'One only!'

There are different opinions about how one can be so many. There are two main schools of thought. One tradition is that all the gods and goddesses are aspects of God, Brahman. They are windows into the mystery of God, each capturing an aspect of God's nature and power. One emphasises creativity, one care, one new life, and so on. Just as a mother can also be a wife, a doctor, and a friend to different people, so God has different aspects.

Try to think of something which is in everything and everywhere but which you cannot see, not even in your mind. That is trying to imagine Brahman. You probably found it impossible. Most people do.

Now think of the sun or the moon. Or look at the pictures in this chapter. That is much easier. So that is how many Hindus think of Brahman. Brahman can take on the form of anything in the world. He may take the shape of a god or goddess. Each god or goddess has its own personality and appearance.

In the form of Brahma, God created the world. (Brahma is one form of Brahman.) As Vishnu, God keeps the world going. And as Shiva, He destroys the world.

Hindus usually have a special feeling about one form of Brahman. They will keep an **image** of their chosen god or goddess in their home. It helps them to concentrate when they worship. Many Hindus choose either Shiva or Vishnu as the god they worship most. A Hindu girl explains what Shiva means to her.

● My favourite god is Shiva, because when we went to India my Mum bought me a necklace and Shiva was on it. I like him because at night, when I have bad thoughts, I think about him and they go away.

Hindus choose a deity as their special image of God to worship, their ishta devata ('chosen way'). They are **devotees** of this god, and will say special prayers, chants, and will wear special markings on their foreheads.

▲ *This priest is a devotee of Vishnu*

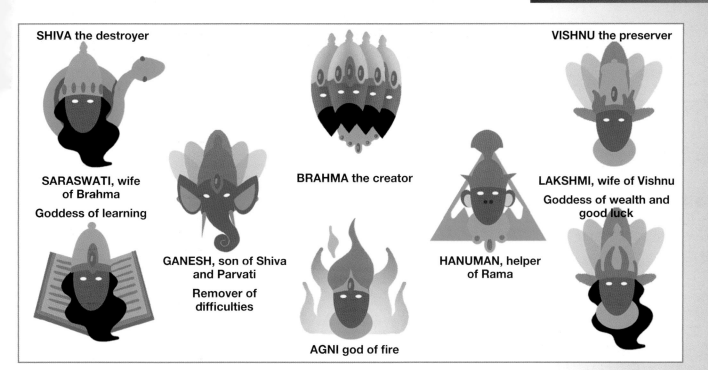

SHIVA the destroyer

SARASWATI, wife of Brahma
Goddess of learning

GANESH, son of Shiva and Parvati
Remover of difficulties

BRAHMA the creator

AGNI god of fire

HANUMAN, helper of Rama

VISHNU the preserver

LAKSHMI, wife of Vishnu
Goddess of wealth and good luck

▲ *Many Hindus say that God can be seen in many forms*

There are also **symbols** which **represent** Brahman. Ones which you can see are a lotus flower and a shining light. The most popular symbol for Brahman is the written and spoken sound Aum.

● Aum means everything, God and the universe. It means all the good things. When you say Aum you don't think of any bad things.

● If you listen carefully to the distant sea waves, you'll hear them chanting Aum. The roaring winds are always chanting Aum. Even when you press a sea-shell against your ear, you'll hear it saying Aum.

Aum represents the sound vibrations of the universe. When we chant it continuously it brings us relaxation, comfort, blessing and peace.

In this book we talk about gods and goddesses, but remember that these are all different forms of the one God, Brahman.

1 There are the names of eight Hindu gods and goddesses in this wordsearch. Write down each one as you find it. Pick any five and write a sentence for each of them.

L	A	G	N	I	B	P	A	H	N
A	C	Q	A	M	H	A	R	B	A
K	G	L	V	N	Y	V	D	S	M
S	R	J	I	T	E	K	N	M	U
H	A	N	H	D	W	S	I	Z	N
M	V	I	S	H	N	U	H	F	A
I	T	A	W	S	A	R	A	S	H

2 a) Is it easy to think about Brahman? Give reasons.

b) How does Hinduism make it easier for its followers to think about God?

c) Why do you think the Hindu girl feels better when she thinks about Shiva?

3 a) Write down any four words or phrases from the list below. Do not choose words which mean the opposite.

strong; beautiful; fierce; wise; sees everything; destroyer; cruel; helpful; creator; brings wealth; brings the weather; helps children.

b) Make up a god or goddess so that the four words or phrases fit him or her. Draw a picture of your idea.

c) Give this god or goddess a name.

d) Explain how you chose this name.

◄ Lord Vishnu seated on cobras, showing his mastery over the forces of chaos

Some Hindus do not see all the deities as being aspects of the one God. They think that only one of them is really God, really an aspect of the Supreme Being, and all the others are lesser gods. The most popular idea is to worship Vishnu as God. He is pictured here with four arms – some see these as representing power – and he usually holds a lotus flower as a symbol of purity and beauty; a discus and a club as weapons and signs of strength, and a **conch** shell. The conch suggests worship – it is blown at the start of a temple service. Some see the one in Vishnu's hand as the song of life, the energy that sustains the universe.

Hindus believe that Vishnu comes to Earth and shows himself as an animal or human form at various times. He comes when evil appears to be triumphant, or when people are irreligious.

> ● Whenever and wherever there is a decline in religious practice ... and a predominant rise of irreligion – at that time I descend Myself. To deliver the pious and to annihilate the miscreants, as well as to establish the principles of religion, I Myself appear, millennium after millennium.
>
> *Gita 4:7–8*

Each birth or appearance of Vishnu is called an 'avatar' (descent of the Lord). Most Hindus believe that there are ten main avatars. Some believe in many others, and some Hindus believe that Jesus is one.

THE TEN AVATARS OF VISHNU

The first six are animal or semi-human in form and the last four are human.

- The fish warned Manu, the Indian version of Noah, about the coming flood.
- The tortoise formed the foundation of the ocean of life when chaos threatened to destroy everything. The ocean of milk was churned which produced many wonderful things such as the moon, and the goddess of Fortune, Lakshmi.
- The boar fought a powerful demon, and rescued the earth as it was pushed under the waters.
- The man-lion killed a demon who ruled the world and forbade people to worship God.
- The dwarf challenged another demon ruler to let him take charge of all the land he could cover with three steps. The demon laughed at his small size and agreed. The dwarf grew to a huge size, and covered the world in two paces, and pushed the demon into the underworld with the third!
- Parasu-rama saved the priests from being killed by the warrior caste.
- Rama defeated the evil king Ravana and rescued his wife, Sita.
- Krishna fought various evil rulers and demons and gave his teachings to Arjuna, which form the Bhagavad Gita.
- The Buddha taught the way to inner peace and enlightenment. (Not all Hindus regard the Buddha as an avatar.)
- Kalki is the avatar yet to come, at the end of our present age. He will bring an age of peace and holiness.

Sometimes, the demon kings are actually human beings who have developed special powers in meditation. They are greedy and selfish and abuse these powers, trying to enslave others. This is a warning to use our gifts wisely.

Some Hindus will only place statues of Vishnu and his avatars (especially Krishna and Rama) in their shrines, or these may be the main shrines. The other deities are seen as 'mahatmas', 'great souls' or as demigods, lesser spiritual beings, perhaps like the saints and angels in Christianity.

Krishna is one of the most popular avatars of Vishnu. He is said to have lived on Earth about five thousand years ago. He was a cow herder, and is often shown playing the flute, with a peacock feather in his hair. Some see the flute as a symbol of heavenly music which he wishes to bring into the world.

1 Draw a comic strip showing the ten avatars of Vishnu in action.
2 Imagine that you are Kalki, arriving on Earth. Describe the changes that you might consider to make the world a better place.
3 Vishnu is often shown with a conch and Krishna with a flute. These suggest God's peace and beauty in the world.
   a) What musical instrument would make you think of peace and beauty?
   b) Talk, in groups, about a piece of music that makes you feel like this. Perhaps some of these could be played in class.

◀ *Rama's battle to rescue Sita*

Bhakti – devotion to a personal God – developed after the lofty, abstract ideas of God in the Upanishads. People want a God to relate to, who can be loved. They want more of a person than a force. In the Middle Ages, various saints danced and sang the praises of Vishnu, and sometimes of Shiva. One of the most influential Vishnu worshippers was Caitanya in Bengal. He lived from 1486 to 1534. He was of a high-caste Brahmin family and he was converted by meeting a devotee of Krishna. He founded a community, some members of which moved to Puri – still a great centre for Krishna worship – and taught that the way to reach oneness with God was by chanting the divine names, 'Hare Krishna, Hare Krishna, Krishna, Krishna, Hare, Hare, Hare Rama, Hare Rama, Rama, Rama, Hare, Hare.' ('Hare' is a name of Radha, Krishna's dearest devotee.) Caitanya taught that Krishna was the supreme God, and that Vishnu was one of his forms. This view is held by the International Society for Krishna Consciousness to this day.

Many of the Bhakti saints protested against the rigid caste system. Many members of the Bhakti communities were from lower castes, and Caitanya once embraced a leper to show his compassion for fellow humans, an act that would have polluted him spiritually in the eyes of the stricter Brahmins.

◄ Caitanya, a Vishnu worshipper from the Middle Ages. This image shows Caitanya in his heavenly state

Some Hindus worship Shiva as the Supreme Lord, rather than Vishnu or Krishna. A verse from one of the later Upanishads shows this:

> ● Love the Lord and be free. He is the One
> Who appears as many, enveloping
> The cosmos, without beginning or end.
> None but the pure in heart can realize him.
> May Lord Shiva, creator, destroyer,
> The abode of all beauty and wisdom,
> Free us from the cycle of birth and death.
> *Shvetashvatara Upanishad*

The dancing figure of Shiva shows his great power over creation. He often holds a flame and a drum, and stands on a demon. The circle is of blazing fire. Some see symbolic meanings in these things:

● The drum is the drum-beat of creation, the rhythm of life.
● The flame is the power to create and to destroy.
● The demon represents ignorance.
● The circle stands for eternity, going round and round.

Hindu teaching on God, and the paths to find union with him, can be summed up by the three terms, Karma, Jnana and Bhakti, understood as action, knowledge and love.

▲ *Lord Shiva*

● God is active, and the source of energy behind all activities. Therefore the fruits of our actions should be offered to God.
● God is the light of true knowledge, guiding the mind, showing the right path to follow through life. As a verse from the *Gita* says, 'Could a thousand suns blaze forth together it would be a faint reflection of the radiance of God'. (*Gita* 11)
● God has a loving relationship with everyone. Those who love God, therefore love all his sons and daughters. God is love, wanting loving praise and service. 'Only by loving service can men see me, and know me, and come unto me.' (*Gita* 11:54)

Likewise, the path to God should include good works, the light of truth and loving worship.

---

1 In groups, write a poem or design a collage called 'The Light of a Thousand Suns'.

2 Talk about a time when the truth has dawned upon you; when you have felt loved; and when you have done something to help someone else.

3 **a)** Work out a role play where Caitanya embraces the leper and strict, religious people tell him off for touching an outcast.

b) What would be regarded as similar in our own society? (For example, Princess Diana did a similar thing with AIDS patients.)

4 List each item in the image of the dancing Shiva and say what these can symbolise.

Hindu ideas about God can be complicated and hard to understand at first. They have many popular stories in works such as the Puranas which teach simple truths in story form.

The Five Blind Men and an Elephant

Five sadhus lived on the banks of the River Indus. They were all blind. One day, a tame elephant wandered to the water's edge and sensed that the men were harmless and gentle. They heard something join them, and they felt around them.

One felt its body, and said it was a wall of mud.

Another felt its tusks and said there were two spears.

One felt the trunk and thought it was a serpent.

Another said it was a piece of rope, as he held its tail.

The last man laughed at them, for he held its leg. He said it was a tree.

A little child walked by and said, 'Why are you all holding the elephant?'

This story is about the mystery of God. It teaches people that when they try to understand God, they can only grasp a part of his nature. It teaches them to remain humble like the little child and not to think they have all the answers or that they can understand everything about God and the universe.

The Butter Thief

Krishna, when a toddler, was being cuddled by his mother. She had been churning butter in a pot and she suddenly remembered that she had left something cooking. She put him down and he pulled over the pot and ate some butter. Then he ran off and fed some to the monkeys. His mother came running, angry and cross. He saw her coming towards him with a stick and he cried. She felt sorry for him, but still wanted to punish him, and so she tried to tie him up. The rope would not reach. Try as she might, it would not meet up and go around his body. She tried a longer rope, but still it would not reach. Eventually, Krishna let himself be tied up, for he realised that his mother was only doing this out of devotion to him, to guide him.

The moral of this story is similar to the last one. People try to capture God and have him all worked out ('tied up') with their minds. They cannot do it. They can only understand what God allows them to, and what he reveals to them about himself. God reveals himself more through love – his devotees capture more of him than all the philosophers and wise men. They cannot come close to understanding Almighty God. If we love God, he will come close to his devotee.

Krishna tries to escape from his mother ▶

32

The Universe in Krishna's Mouth

The child Krishna played with the other boys and girls of his village, and often teased the adults by stealing butter, or untying the cows. More often than not, he would play in the mud with his brother. One day, the village children told his mother that he had eaten dirt. Krishna denied this. 'Open your mouth, then, and let me see!' said his mother. When he did so, she saw the whole universe within, the spinning galaxies and the blazing sun. Then his mother realised that this was God, Vishnu, in human form. She bowed down and worshipped him, but then Krishna made her lose all memory of what had happened and she took him on her knee and loved him.

The moral of this story is that seemingly small and insignificant things can hide great truths. People can find God within the small, ordinary things of life. God is Almighty and vast. But if people draw close to God in love, they are not frightened or overawed, but find trust and acceptance.

Krishna the Cowherd Boy

Krishna was a cow-herder as a youth, and he played games with the other boys as they took the cows to the river. They imitated monkeys, frogs and peacocks, dressing up and hopping around. After hours of roaming around, they were tired. Then, Krishna took out his bamboo flute and started to play. The music was so beautiful that the river ran backwards, birds fell from the sky in a trance, and the calves stood as though frozen. The music stopped, and all went back to normal, but now, there was no question of tiredness. They all opened their lunch and shared this out, spreading it out on rocks and palm leaves in the forest.

The moral of this story is that God is beautiful and full of life. His wonderful beauty draws people to him in devotion. Once smitten by the love of God, the devotee's mind is stolen by him. All other pleasures become insignificant.

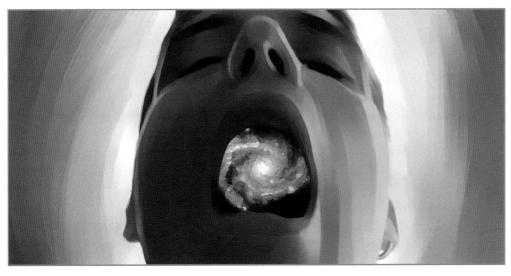

▲ *All of the vast universe in the child Krishna's mouth*

1 Act out the story of the blind men and the elephant. Have a narrator saying what the moral is.

2 In what way can people try to tie up God? Why are we doomed to fail?

3 How does belief in avatars explain the story of the universe in Krishna's mouth?

4 a) Think of the most beautiful things you have ever seen. Talk about these.

b) If you felt God's presence, would it feel any less beautiful? Discuss.

c) What does Krishna's flute playing symbolise?

The Rasa Dance

One moonlit night, Krishna played beautiful music on his flute. The Gopis, the cow-herd girls, were milking the cows, serving their families, or bathing, when they heard the music. They stopped whatever they were doing and ran into the forest. They found Krishna by the riverside, and they danced, joked and talked with him. One by one, girls began to feel proud that they were with Krishna. It was then that Krishna disappeared. Heartbroken, they searched everywhere. They begged the very trees to reveal where he was hiding! They imitated Krishna's flute playing, and acted like him, to console themselves. Two sets of footprints were found. One belonged to Krishna, and the other to his favourite, Radha. They felt sad and even a little jealous. Later, only Radha's footprints could be seen. Krishna had even abandoned her. They found her a little way ahead, weeping. They had all been too proud, and they confessed their fault and chanted Krishna's name. Then Krishna appeared in among them, smiling. He started a dance, and multiplied himself, so that each Gopi danced with a form of himself. Under the light of the moon, the forest animals crept out of hiding to watch the beautiful dance, known as the Rasa dance.

The moral of the story is that God withdraws his presence when people become proud. God delights to be in our lives, but cannot be where evil lives. Sometimes, having a blessing from God can initially help people, but then make them proud. We have to be careful to remember that we are all nothing without the love and help of God.

Krishna and the Gopis

One day the Gopi girls were bathing in the river. They had worshipped and prayed that Krishna would be their husband, offering beautiful flowers, sprigs of fresh leaves, fruits, rice and fragrant perfumes. Krishna was with the boys of his own age, and he decided to play a trick upon the girls. He stole their clothes as they were bathing and hid with them in a tree. The boys laughed as they watched the girls sink up to their necks in the water to avoid being seen. Krishna called them out, one by one, to present themselves before him. Embarrassed, they did so, covering up their bodies with their hands. He asked them to place their hands together on their heads, in the attitude of worship, and then to bow at his feet. They worshipped him like this, and he placed their clothes on their shoulders. Their shame was soon overcome by joy, for they were the object of Krishna's delight, and his brides, as they desired.

The moral of this story is that we cannot hide anything from God. The Gopis are seen as each person's soul, standing spiritually naked before God. The story teaches that God will then fulfil our desires if they are pure.

Many Hindus believe these stories are based upon facts, with symbolic meanings. Some treat them just as symbols.

Some of these stories have God being naughty and playful. Is this surprising? Hindus see this as meaning that God wants to challenge us and that sometimes suffering can make us better people.

1 a) Why do you think Krishna left the Gopis when they became proud?
  b) Think of a time when someone saw right through you, and you had to be yourself with them. How did this feel?
  c) What does it mean for the soul to be naked before God?

◄ Krishna appeared with each Gopi and danced with them

◀ Life is like a journey . . .

Life is like a journey. We grow, develop, change and go to new places. We learn new skills. We grow into adulthood, possibly marry, have children, grow old and die one day. Time passes, things change.

None of us knows what lies ahead. A wise saying states, 'Life is what happens to you while you are making other plans.'

Some cultures and faiths have special ceremonies for different stages along life's journey, like marriage or a funeral. Every culture has a way of celebrating a baby's birth, and many have a ceremony to mark the end of childhood, and the start of adulthood. These ceremonies are called rites of passage. They are like milestones along the road of life, marking the passage from one stage to another.

The Hindu holy books say that a person's life is like a journey. On the way, sixteen important steps are taken. These are called samskaras. They begin even before a child is **conceived** in the mother's womb. Religious ceremonies mark some of these samskaras.

35

1 Brainstorm on how life is like a journey. Collect all the ideas on a large sheet of paper and display this.
2 Draw a path of some kind (road/railway/space journey?) and mark on special things that have happened to you so far. These could be birthdays, holidays, presents, trips or people you have met. You might include sad things like a pet's death, or a stay in hospital, too. Be creative – use your imagination in the drawing.
3 **a)** Which steps on life's journey would you like a special ceremony for? Why?
   b) In groups, create some ceremonies for stages of life that you do not have already, such as coming of age.

● Birth and Childhood

When a baby is born, the parents tell the priest. He finds out the positions of the planets and **constellations** at the exact time of the birth. He prepares a **horoscope** for the baby. He does this because many Hindus believe that the stars and planets influence a person's life. The priest uses the horoscope to tell the parents which letter the baby's name should begin with.

But not all Hindus choose their children's names in this way. This Hindu mother in England explains why.

> ● We are supposed to have the first letter from a horoscope, but we didn't. I didn't know anybody like a priest who could cast a horoscope. So I just picked names that would be easy to spell and to pronounce.

Hindu babies are often named after gods or goddesses, such as Krishna or Lakshmi. Some other names are Rani (princess) or Pooja (worship), for a girl, and Vishal (mighty) or Deepak (light) for a boy.

▲ The first haircut – one of the early samskaras

10 Sacred Thread

Aum. Let us meditate on the glorious light of the creator. May he guide our minds

9 First Haircut

May bad things be cut out of your life

8 Ears Pierced

7 *You eat food with the indrawing breath*

6 *Feel the sunlight for the first time*

5 *Your name is Ramesh*

4 *May your name and words be as sweet as honey all your life*

3 *May my growing child feel my calmness*

2 *May this food help my growing child to be healthy*

1 *May we have a child to love and bring up to live a good life*

▲ The samskaras of childhood

The Sacred Thread

An exciting day for many young Hindu boys comes some time between their eighth and eleventh birthdays. It is the tenth samskara, when they are given the **sacred** thread. Only boys who belong to the three highest varnas can wear it.

The thread is made from three strands of cotton: white, red or yellow. These remind the wearer of his duties:

- to God for giving him everything he needs
- to his parents for giving birth to him
- to his religious teacher for all he has taught him.

Some Hindus believe the strands stand for the three main gods, Brahma, Vishnu and Shiva. Others say they are to remind them to control what they think, say and do.

The ceremony takes place at home. The priest or religious teacher puts the thread on. It goes over the boy's left shoulder and under his right arm. He wears it all his life, though it is changed regularly, once a year.

The sacred thread ceremony is like a second birth; it is the beginning of the spiritual path. The boy is now thought of as an adult, too. But boys do not have to take the sacred thread.

This mother in England explains why her two sons have not.

> ● Our boys have not taken the thread because they eat meat. In these things, I think you have to stick to everything. If they take the thread they have to give up meat. I don't want to force them. It's something they must choose.

◄ *The sacred thread ceremony*

---

1 Copy out and complete this paragraph. There are _____ important steps in a Hindu's life. Each step is called a _____ . The first one takes place before _____ . At the tenth step, boys receive a _____ _____ . They are now thought of as _____ .

2 **a)** Why do you think Hindus say life is like a journey?

b) Which samskara is shown in the photograph on page 37? Explain how you decided.

c) Write a sentence about three important steps in your life so far. For each one, explain why it was important.

3 **a)** Why do you think parents may name a baby after a god or goddess?

b) Which god or goddess would you like to be named after? Give reasons.

4 People claim to be able to tell the future in many ways. Would you like to know your future?

● Marriage

Choosing the person you marry will be one of the biggest decisions of your life. If you make the right choice, you will want to stay with that person until one of you dies. But an unwise choice could cause a great deal of unhappiness.

Hindus believe it is their duty to marry. Then their children will be able to carry on the family's religious traditions. But they also believe that young people may easily choose the wrong person. So Hindu marriages are usually arranged by the parents.

The idea is that the parents choose someone who is like their son or daughter in upbringing, education and varna. If a couple shares these things, there is a good chance that they will get on well together. Love will come gradually.

Hindu parents today, especially in Britain, are not always as strict as their parents and grandparents used to be. Then, marriages may have been arranged when the son and daughter were children. The couple themselves would have no say in the matter at all. And sometimes the bride would not see the groom until the wedding day.

Today parents usually allow the couple to meet each other first. Either of them can refuse if they wish to. A Hindu boy describes what happened in his family.

> When my sister got married, that was arranged. My whole family went to his house first. We met his parents and his family. Then we went home and we phoned them afterwards to tell them what we thought. They said, 'Yes' and we said, 'Yes'.
>
> So my sister got married. The groom sat on the stage. He wore a garland of flowers. People threw money on the stage and they collected it all for the bride and groom.
>
> When my brother gets married, I'm going to have to sit on the stage with him all the time. I have to give him support.

This Hindu woman remembers her nephew's wedding in Southampton.

> The bridegroom sat in front of the procession on a horse. They have to have something covering their face and they should sit on a horse. Not everybody in England does, but he was the only son, so they had the proper ceremony.
>
> There was a party. They had the Salvation Army band as well. There was dancing in the hall.
>
> Nobody had drink. We're not supposed to have drink. But nowadays, children born here are a bit different. They say, 'When we go to our friends' marriages and parties, they have drinks.' So sometimes you have to go along with that.

▶ This Hindu bride is ready for her wedding. She has bathed in water perfumed with rose water. The most important ladies on her family have rubbed her skin with oil and **turmeric** *powder. This purifies her skin and makes it glow.*

Her **sari** *and her jewels are the best her family can afford. She wears jewels on her head, and bracelets of gold and ivory. The red patterns on her hands are made with* **henna**. *They will last for many weeks. They are symbols of her entry into a new life.*

The family's priest has cast the horoscopes of the bride and groom. This has helped him to fix the best date for the wedding. Now the important night has arrived.

Hindu weddings often take place at night, when the pole star comes out. This is because the promises the bride and groom make to each other are like the pole star. They will never change.

After the ceremony, the bride and groom sometimes put their handprints on the wall of the bride's home. This will remind her family of her when she has left

▲ *A newly married Hindu couple*

At a Hindu wedding, seven steps are taken round the sacred fire. These steps symbolise hopes the couple have for their marriage. They are

- food,
- energy,
- wealth,
- happiness,
- children,
- seasons, and
- friendship.

When a scarf is tied and carried, this symbolises the joining of their lives in marriage. After the last step they are husband and wife.

The sacred fire represents the presence of God, pure, powerful and unable to be touched.

Note the rice grains which are offered, and sprinked over the bride and groom. These represent fertility – another Indian custom adopted in the West.

1 Match the symbols in List A with their meanings in List B.

List A
- patterns on hands and feet
- handprints on wall
- fourth step
- pole star
- final step

List B
- promises will never change
- happiness
- reminder of bride
- friendship
- beginning new life

2 Write the words from the list below which you think describe a Hindu wedding. Give reasons for each word you choose, quoting the Hindu boy or woman if you can.
happy; sad; short; serious; quiet; symbolic; colourful; lively; long; expensive; boring; religious.

3 a) Write down two things from this chapter which show that some Hindus are not as strict as others.
  b) Suggest reasons for this.

4 a) Why do Hindu parents usually arrange their sons' and daughters' marriages?
  b) In groups, note down reasons for or against this idea. Share your ideas with the rest of the class.

● Old Age and Death

Hindus usually spend the rest of their lives as householders. They bring up their families, go to work and live as part of the community. But some Hindu men begin to take less part in everyday life so that they can think more about God. They may become religious teachers.

This is the fourteenth step. It takes place after a Hindu's children have grown up and married. Now he can retire and live quietly. He spends much of his time praying and reading holy books. Often he lives in one of his sons' homes. Sometimes, in India, he will go away and live in the forest or go on a long pilgrimage. His wife may go with him or he may go alone.

A few Hindus may finally give up everything (home, wife, possessions) and become a sanyasi. It means 'one who has given up everything'. He may also be referred to as a sadhu – a saintly person. A sanyasi may wander around the countryside with only a cloth round his waist, a food bowl and a water pot.

Very occasionally, a Hindu will decide to become a sadhu when he is young. So he will never marry, go to work or own anything. A sadhu hopes that he may gain Moksha, as this one explains.

● By worshipping daily and living a sadhu's life, the result is you meet God himself. God takes a sadhu and that man is freed from coming and going. He will not have to be reborn into human form again.

There are many sadhus who don't attach importance to anybody. For twenty-four hours of the day they think only of God. They don't worry about food and drink. God comes down and feeds them.

Some go a little way, some go half-way, some cross over completely [to God]. And some who sing praises day and night never cross over. I hope that I will cross over. But it is in God's hands.

40

◀ *A Hindu sadhu in Nepal*

When a Hindu dies, his or her body is washed. It is dressed in new clothes, and flowers are put round it. The whole family shows its respect by bringing flowers and touching the dead person's feet.

The sixteenth samskara is **cremation**. In India, the body is burned on a funeral **pyre**. The fire should be lit by the dead person's eldest son. The fire helps the soul to move on to its new destination. The ashes are scattered in a holy river. Many cremations take place by the River Ganges. Hindus believe that if they die near the Ganges they will escape rebirth. In Britain, the ceremony takes place in a **crematorium**. At the end of the ceremony, the priest chants the final prayer.

> ● The soul is never born, and never dies.
>   Once living, it never ceases to live.
>   As a man lays aside his worn-out clothes
>   And puts on others that are new
>   So the soul within the body lays aside that body
>   And puts on another body that is new.
>   May your eyes return to the sun, and your breath to
>   the wind, your waters to the ocean and your ashes to
>   the earth from whence they came.

▲ *The funeral pyre is lit by the eldest son*

This teenager remembers how he felt after his grandfather's death.

> ● When it came to my turn [to touch his feet], I
>   remembered how fond **Dadaji** had been of us, his
>   grandchildren, and I felt very upset.
>   But we must not be too sad about Dadaji's death.
>   His life had been a good one, and we feel sure that his
>   [soul] will gain a good rebirth.

The bodies of babies and saints are not always cremated at death, because they are considered sinless. Saints are sometimes buried and a baby's body may be tied to a heavy stone and lowered into the middle of the river. A light, symbol of the baby's soul, may later be sent downstream.

1 **a)** What is the fourteenth step for a Hindu?
  b) At what time of his life may he take that step?
  c) Why do you think he might decide not to take it?
2 **a)** What is a sadhu?
  b) What is a sadhu's aim?
  c) Do you think a sadhu's life is easy? Give your reasons.
  d) Some Sadhus choose to live in caves. Why do you think this is?
  e) Do you think there are many sadhus in Britain? Give reasons.
3 **a)** Why do you think Hindus want to die by the River Ganges?
  b) Read the funeral prayer. What do you think are the *worn-out clothes* of the soul?
  c) What will the soul's new clothes be?
  d) Write your own funeral prayer for a baby. Include a part about the light.
4 Do you believe you have a soul? If yes, what do you think happens to it at death? If not, give reasons.

Everyone looks forward to going on holiday. We may hope to make new friends and visit interesting places. But we often have to do without things beforehand so that we can afford it. And sometimes there's first a long, uncomfortable journey.

Pilgrimages are a bit like this. People go on them so they can worship at special places connected with their religion. For Hindus, the journey is both a religious event and an opportunity to meet other people.

Hindus enjoy their pilgrimages because they are doing their religious duty. They do not laze on the beach or dance in clubs or eat out in restaurants.

Most pilgrimages end at a temple. Out of the hundreds of temples, Hindus have twelve that are especially important. Four of these, at Badrinath, Rameshwaram, Puri and Dwarka, are the most important.

Every Hindu would really like to be able to visit each one of these four. But they are thousands of miles apart. This means that poor Hindus need to save up for a long time. Even then, the pilgrimage will not be easy.

But the difficulties are worth it. They are a way of showing how much Hindus can put up with in order to worship God. And it is not only poor people who have a hard time, as this pilgrim explains.

> ● A rich person might go barefoot. He might be **scantily** dressed, even in very cold weather. The idea is that we have to forget too much comfort. We undertake a bit of suffering. Then, through our own suffering, we are able to realise and understand other people's suffering as well.

Thus pilgrims accept difficulties voluntarily for the sake of spiritual advancement.

The temple at Badrinath is visited by many pilgrims ▶

Many rivers and mountains are places of pilgrimage. The Ganges is the holiest river of all. Hindus call it Mother Ganga. All Hindus would like to go to bathe in this river. They believe it will wash away all their sins. Many Hindu writers have praised the Ganges. Here is what one said:

> ● O, Mother Ganga, I bow down to you. By a mere touch of your holy waters, even snakes, horses, deer and monkeys (not to mention human beings) become as pure and as beautiful as Shiva. They can then wander about unafraid.

Pooja and Anuj went to the Ganges:

> ● Pooja: It comes from the Himalayas, the snow mountains. The snow melts and comes down.
>
> ● Anuj: It's a river from Heaven. Shiva brought it down to wash all the sins away. You get pure again.

This is how another Hindu described his pilgrimage to Varanasi. Varanasi is a holy city on the banks of the Ganges. It is sometimes called Benares.

> ● I felt there might be just a few people there seeking after God. But when I went there I saw so many people. Thousands of people, early in the morning. Getting up when most people in the rest of the world would be in their beds.
>
> When I went there I had my first bath in the Ganges. I was really thrilled that I was able to bathe in this sacred river, this river that so many people had bathed in. It was a really tremendous feeling, a feeling of relief, a feeling of joy. It was like going to Heaven.

◀ *Pilgrims bathing in the River Ganges*

1 Match the words in List A with their meanings in List B.

List A	List B
• Varanasi	• an important temple
• pilgrimage	• where the Ganges begins
• Mother Ganga	• a holy city
• Himalayas	• a religious journey
• Puri	• the holiest river

2 a) Copy the map on page 4.

b) Put a cross (X) on the map to mark the four most important Hindu temples.

c) Use an atlas to work out roughly how far a Hindu would have to travel to visit all four.

d) What do you think would be the problems of pilgrimage for Hindus living in India?

e) What extra problems would there be if you live in Britain?

3 a) Describe at least three ways in which pilgrims are prepared to suffer.

b) How do you think this helps them to feel they are doing their religious duty?

c) Describe an occasion when you might deliberately make something difficult for yourself. Give your reasons for doing it.

At Jagannath, in Puri, Krishna is worshipped in the form of a huge image which is driven around during the festival in a huge chariot. 'Jagannath' gives us the word 'juggernaut'. Decorated elephants follow the chariot, with a procession of sadhus. It is a carnival atmosphere, and to see the image of the deity is to receive his blessing.

An old Hindu story reveals a great deal about Hindu attitudes to worship.

Jagannath is worshipped daily by pilgrims who make offerings of food at his temple. One day, a wealthy merchant visited the shrine and thought the deity was nothing more than a painted statue with black face and large eyes. He thought he would tease the temple priests.

'I would like to offer one hundred thousand rupees to cover the cost of one food offering. But this is only on one condition, that every last rupee is used.'

The priests were overwhelmed, but then they thought more about it. Even using the most expensive foods, much of the money would be left over. The priests prayed to Jagannath for wisdom, and asked the merchant to stay until they had their answer. Three days later, the head priest had a dream. Then he went to see the merchant.

'Lord Jagannath says that you should pay for one betel leaf and nut and have it mashed into a paste as an offering,' said the priest.

'But . . . is that all?' asked the bewildered merchant.

'No . . . the leaf must be smeared with powder from a finely ground pearl,' replied the priest.

'That is more like it!' said the merchant.

'But it must be a very rare pearl found under the skin of a certain elephant's forehead,' came the reply.

The merchant was furious. He would have to spend thousands of rupees to buy elephants before he found one with such a rare pearl. He threw down his turban and said, 'I am not even able to offer a single nut to Lord Jagannath!'

Slowly, his anger faded, and he realised how foolish he had been. He ran to the temple room, threw himself on the floor before Jagannath and begged for forgiveness.

'Everything belongs to you, so what can I possibly offer? The only thing I have is my heart!'

From that day on the merchant was a changed man, using his wealth to feed the poor.

In the Gita, Krishna says, 'If one offers Me with love and devotion a leaf, a flower, fruit, or water, I will accept it.' (9:26)

▲ *Hindus in Britain celebrate the Jagannath festival*

1 a) Draw Jagannath in his chariot.
   b) Imagine that you are a pilgrim. You want a blessing by seeing the deity. What might this be?
2 a) Draw a comic strip of the story of the proud merchant.
   b) What is the moral of this story?
   c) Make a classroom display of the offerings of leaves, flowers, fruit and a bowl of water. Write poems about the things these things suggest, and write out Krishna's saying in decorative text.

◄ *Rangoli pictures are made with coloured powder. Here, one of the deities is represented*

Most religions celebrate special events with festivals or sacred holidays. People thank God for the wonderful things He has given them and join with other members of their religion in traditional rituals.

The two main reasons for Hindu festivals are:
- to celebrate events in the lives of various deities and of holy people
- to mark the changing seasons.

The Hindu calendar is worked out according to the changes in the moon. This means dates do not exactly match those in the Western calendar, which is based solely on the sun. So Hindu festivals come on slightly different dates each year according to the Western calendar.

Hinduism probably has more holidays than any other religion, although not all Hindus take part in every festival. People celebrate in different ways in different places. The same festival can last between one and five days, depending where it is held.

Hindus may remember stories about different gods even though the festival has the same name.

The official Hindu New Year is at the beginning of the Indian summer, in March or April. But in some parts of India, New Year is celebrated at other times! It is a good day to start something new, like going to school or a different job.

Some Hindu families make a special banner to welcome the New Year. They tie a piece of new cloth, a cooking pot, some pieces of sugar and a leafy branch to a bamboo pole. They fix this to a doorpost and tie fresh flowers to it. Each item stands for something they hope God will give them during the New Year.

The holy books say that Hindus should make Rangoli at New Year. These are patterns on the ground outside their houses. They are made with coloured powdered stone and rice powder. The patterns may be of Hindu symbols or words of greeting. They are to welcome the New Year and to greet visitors.

45

1 Look at the Hindu calendar on page 46.

a) Make a list of the main Hindu festivals in the order they take place. Start with New Year. Use a new line for each.

b) Next to each festival, write the season in which it takes place.

2 a) Make a list of things which may go on a Hindu New Year banner.

b) Write down what you think each item stands for.

c) Write down four things which you might wish for at the beginning of the year.

d) Draw your own New Year banner. Include an item which stands for each of your New Year wishes.

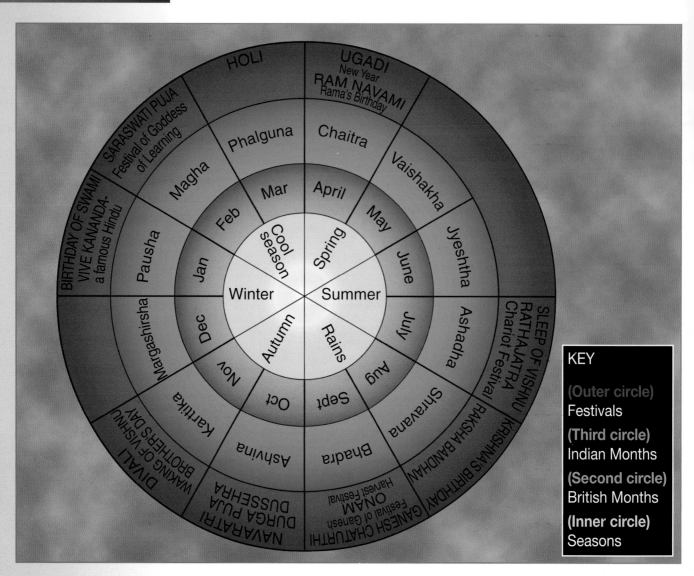

Calendar wheel labels (from image):

HOLI

UGADI — New Year
RAM NAVAMI — Rama's Birthday

SARASWATI PUJA — Festival of Goddess of Learning

BIRTHDAY OF SWAMI VIVE KANANDA - a famous Hindu

SLEEP OF VISHNU
RATHAJATRA — Chariot Festival
KRISHNA'S BIRTHDAY
RAKSHA BANDHAN

DIVALI
WAKING OF VISHNU
BROTHERS DAY
KARTIKA
NAVARATRI
DURGA PUJA
DASSEHRA
ONAM — Harvest Festival
GANESH CHATURTHI — Festival of Ganesh

Indian Months (third circle): Phalguna, Chaitra, Vaishakha, Jyeshtha, Ashadha, Shravana, Bhadra, Ashvina, Kartika, Margashirsha, Pausha, Magha

British Months (second circle): Mar, April, May, June, July, Aug, Sept, Oct, Nov, Dec, Jan, Feb

Seasons (inner circle): Cool season, Spring, Summer, Rains, Autumn, Winter

KEY
(Outer circle) Festivals
(Third circle) Indian Months
(Second circle) British Months
(Inner circle) Seasons

▲ *The Hindu calendar, showing the most popular festivals*

● Brothers and Sisters

There are two festivals for brothers and sisters. Bhratri Dwitiya means Brothers' Day. Brothers and sisters give each other presents and the family has a special meal. The girl prays that her brothers will live for a long time. She rubs **sandalwood** powder onto their foreheads. As she does this, she chants a prayer:

> ● With this, I pray God to save you from any disease and accidental death. May your life be full of golden future.

The other festival is Raksha Bandhan. The wicked king Bali drove the god Indra out of his kingdom. Vishnu gave Indra's wife a thread to put on Indra's wrist. It brought him luck. So he was able to defeat Bali and get his kingdom back.

This is what happens in Hindu families today.

> ● I take a bracelet made of string. It's got a flower on it. I put it on my brother's wrist and he keeps it on for about a week. I give my brother some sweets and he gives me some money. He is promising to look after me. I suppose he might buy me what I want and protect me from bullies.

1 a) Write down three ways in which a brother can protect his sister.

b) Do you think it is a good idea for a brother to promise to protect his sister? Give reasons.

Rama and Ravana

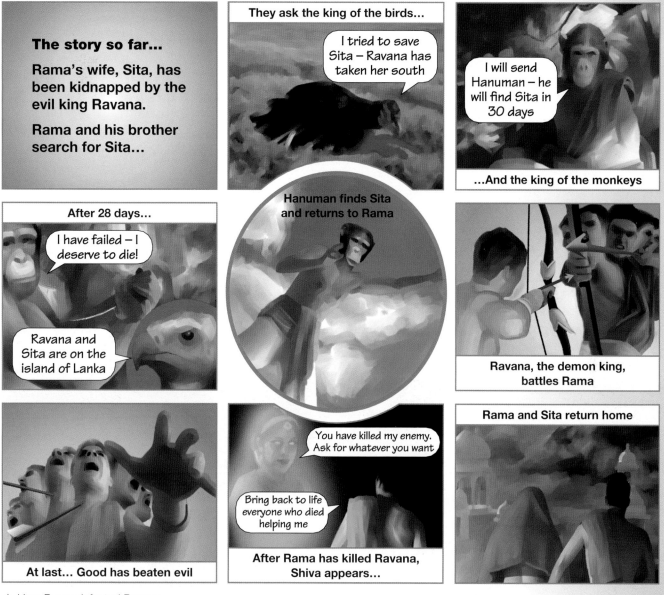

▲ *How Rama defeated Ravana*

Dassehra is the day to remember the story of Rama. Madhur Jaffrey, a famous Hindu writer and cook, describes the festival:

> • All this happened thousands of years ago but even today the story is acted out in every city and village in India. It is a nationwide celebration of the victory of Good over Evil.
>
> In our family, we children would make rough clay statues of the demon, Ravana, and then lay them down on our driveway. Shouting 'Kill, kill, kill,' we would hop onto our bicycles and ride all over the statues, crushing them to pieces.

Often, a huge paper statue of Ravana is burned. It is filled with fireworks, so there will be plenty of noise.

● Divali

The word Divali means a row of lights. The festival takes place on the darkest nights of late autumn. It lasts between two and five days. Different stories and ideas are connected with it.

Hindus put rows of oil lamps or Divas along their window ledges or outside the door. They may remember how Rama was welcomed home after he defeated Ravana. Also, the light may be to show Lakshmi the way to their houses. Here is Madhur Jaffrey, again.

> ● Nothing was lit until after the evening prayers – and after my mother had told us the Divali story. We would run outside and begin lighting the lamps.
>
> Soon the whole house would be glittering, as would our neighbour's house and the house next to that. The whole country was probably glittering. Then it was time for the fireworks. My father would aim a fiery rocket towards the sky. I would take a long sparkler, stand in the middle of the lawn and then turn round and round and round until I seemed encircled by my own glow.

Whichever story is told, it includes light. Light is the opposite of darkness. And good is the opposite of evil. So the Divali lights stand for the victory of good over evil.

▲ *A house lit up at Divali*

Holi

Holi is a spring festival. It is also a time when Hindus celebrate events in the lives of the main deities. It is named after the evil Princess Holika. She planned to kill her nephew in a bonfire. In the end she died in the fire instead.

The festival begins on the night of the full moon and lasts for up to five days. In the evening, the priest lights a huge bonfire. This is known as burning Holi. Often men and boys dance round the fire. Some of them may even try to jump over it. Hindus believe the Holi bonfire is especially sacred.

One of the most popular events celebrated is about Krishna. He was playing with some boys and girls in the village where he lived. As a joke, he started throwing water and coloured powder over his friends. Everyone got very excited and joined in the fun.

So, on the morning after the Holi bonfire, Hindus pelt everyone with coloured powder and water and play practical jokes. It's called playing Holi. Nobody is safe. Children can be cheeky to adults in the family without being told off. Even the most serious people can let themselves go and join in the noisy celebrations. Madhur Jaffrey explains:

- Holi is a leveller, and there was no one we wanted to level more than those against whom we held **grudges**. A special ugly colour was prepared for them. We combined grease with mud, slime and purple dye. The **concoction** would be reserved for our enemies. For our best friends, we prepared a golden paint, carefully mixing real gilt and oil in a small jar.

In the afternoon it is time for a bath! Luckily, the colour usually washes out easily. Then everyone puts on clean clothes. Now they are ready for a special festival meal.

▲ *Young people throw dye over each other at Holi*

These are just some of the most important Hindu festivals. There are many, many more. Each god and goddess has his or her own special day, and many villages have festivals connected with local events or places.

Most of them are linked to stories. It is a way of teaching people about their religion, and many Hindu stories are about someone good defeating someone evil. They help people to understand that, even though there are good and bad things in the world, there is always a way to make their own lives better. More importantly, these stories turn people's minds to God and encourage them to worship him.

49

---

1 **a)** Act out the story of Rama and Ravana in class.
  b) Design your own idea of an evil power – use traditional images like skulls, and modern ones.
  c) Make up your own story of good winning over evil. Act out one of these in class.
2 Imagine you are a Hindu youth. Write a letter telling a friend what you do at Holi.
3 Think up a levelling game that you could try out at school, or in your neighbourhood. What would you have people doing? How might they react?

▲ *A Hindu family shrine inside the home*

Many people like to have a place where they can go to be quiet and think. Your parents may have somewhere they go to get away from you! Hindus like to have a place to pray or think about God.

Of course, there are the temples. But a Hindu does not have to visit a temple. The home is the centre of a Hindu family's religious life. So every Hindu home has a **shrine** for worship. If the house is large enough, it may be a separate room. Or it may simply be a shelf or a corner in any room. A Hindu girl describes her house:

> ● We've got a shrine which my Dad made – a little one. We put a candle in it and my Mum sings a holy song. Everybody sits down and starts praying. Then my Mum sings again.

There are always images or pictures of the family's chosen deity or deities in the shrine. Hindus often put lights in front of them, and they are decorated with shiny things like tinsel.

The woman of the home usually takes care of the shrine. In the morning she carries out a ritual called puja. First she wakes the deity by lighting a lamp. Some women wash and dress the image. Next she offers flowers and burns incense. Finally, she offers food.

A woman and girl explain this.

> ● I take the food and put it on a plate in front of our household god. I do ritual sprinkling with water and leave the god's part there. I take part of the offering back as prashad or blessed food. I mix this in with the food for the family.
>
> ● God gives us food, so we just imagine that we're giving God a welcome by offering food. It's a way of saying, 'Thank you for everything you've done'. Prashad is holy food that's been given to God. After He's eaten it we can eat. It's quite rude to eat before God does.

Hindus believe their bodies should be clean before they worship. They bathe or shower every morning and put on clean clothes. In India, many Hindus go first thing in the morning to bathe in the nearest river.

They try to pray at least three times a day. Then, they feel that their minds are clean.

They mostly offer two kinds of prayer. The first praises God for the very gift of life itself. The second asks God for something they want. It may be for help because they are in trouble. Or for the recovery of someone who is ill. They may also ask for **liberation**, or to become a better person with the strength and wisdom to serve God better. Pooja and her mother explain:

> ● I just tell them, when they get up, pray to God, let us do good things and be kind to people. Don't let's do mean things. Give us a good day. At night when you go to bed . . .
>
> ● Pooja: . . . you close your eyes and say Aum three times. Then you are quiet for five minutes and say Aum again. Then I feel tired and peaceful.

Hindus choose their prayers from their holy books. They chant the Gayatri **mantra** at morning puja. The worship often ends with these words:

> ● Peace be in the heavens; peace be on Earth. May the waters flow peacefully. May the herbs and shrubs grow peacefully. May all the divine powers bring us peace. And may that peace come to us. Aum. Peace. Peace. Peace.

Performing puja is not the only way to worship. Sometimes Hindus just sit quietly and read from the Scriptures. Or they may chant one of the many names of God. Often they start the day with yoga or **meditation**.

At the end of the day, the mother performs puja again. The image is laid down for the night. But, as this Hindu mother explains:

> ● We must not forget our God for a single minute. If we are in trouble and remember our God, we feel peace in our minds. We are busy doing everything, our dusting or our cooking. But if we want peace, we remember we are doing it for God.

▲ *Puja at home. In some families the father performs the ceremony*

1 Explain the meaning of each of these words: shrine; puja, prashad; yoga; mantra.
2 **a)** Why do Hindus offer food to the gods?
  b) What is meant by prashad?
  c) Do you think prashad tastes different from ordinary food? Give your reasons.
  d) Write down two other ways in which Hindus show that their gods are important.
3 **a)** What are the two main reasons Hindus say prayers?
  b) Imagine that you are a Hindu. Write your own prayer. Include:
    (i) something you wish to say thank you for
    (ii) something you want. Explain why it is important for you to have it.
4 Design a 'Thank you' box. Decorate a box with colourful paper or your artwork. Inside the box place photos, objects, letters – anything that reminds you of things you want to give thanks for in life.

Some young people were asked to design their ideal space for worship in their homes. Some imagined a quiet place in the garden, the loft or a shed. One girl said how she would sit on bean bags, light floating candles, burn incense and listen to ambient music, with the lights dimmed.

'This would make me feel relaxed, and peaceful. Then, I might feel spiritual!'

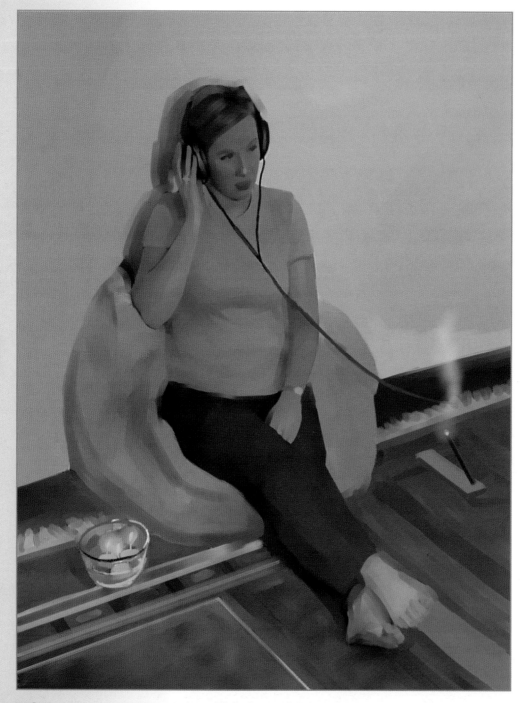

▲ *Chill out! Incense, ambient music and flickering candlelight*

1 Explain what all the items are used for in an act of puja.
2 Design your ideal worship space in your home.
3 Make up a mantra that you would like to chant, such as 'Peace, be still.'

A Hindu temple is the home of God or a particular god or goddess. Each temple has a shrine with an image of its particular deity. There may also be smaller shrines, too.

Temples vary in size. In some villages you might find a simple hut with an image inside. Most temples in India are grand and ornate.

The priest takes care of the deity which he wakes up and washes. Next, food is offered and then the deity is dressed in beautiful clothes, ready for the worshippers. They come to pray and to view the deity.

Hindus take off their shoes before they go into the main part of the temple. Some wash their hands, too. Visiting the deity is like going to see a friend whom you respect. Worshippers ring a bell to tell the deity they have arrived. The bell rings repeatedly as more and more people arrive.

Most of the time, Hindus pray on their own or with their families. Everyone gets together for special occasions like weddings or festivals.

Hindus stand or sit on the floor to pray. Sometimes they put their hands together. And prayers do not have to be silent. Some Hindus pray aloud or sing their messages to the deity. Some play musical instruments to accompany their prayers. A temple can be a noisy place!

Cymbals clash, stringed instruments and wind instruments play, and some people clap or dance along. Worship is serious at times, but can also be joyful. The presence of God is to be enjoyed, for it is beautiful to Hindus. There will be times of silent prayer and meditation, or listening to the Scriptures, but otherwise there are many different things to do.

Lively worship in a temple – singing, drumming, ringing bells. Praise is to be joyful ▶

▲ *A priest performs the Arti ceremony*

A Hindu man and his daughter explain the importance of fire.

- God is in the form of divine light, The fire, you know, is a very holy holy fire. It can purify everything and that is why it is lit.

- You almost touch the flame with your hand, and then you just bring your hands to your head. That's a blessing from God. It's as if God is actually in the flame and he's giving you the blessing.

After praying, a Hindu makes an offering of flowers, food or money. The priest places it in front of the image. No gift is too small, as Lord Krishna says in the Gita:

- If one offers Me with love and devotion a leaf, a flower, a fruit or water I will accept it.

Food and flowers might be brought as offerings. The priest gives out prashad – blessed food – to the worshippers in return.

The deity rests in the afternoon, so the temple is closed for a time. In the evening, the priest prepares the deity for the night.

This might sound strange to Western ears, but Hindus make the images carefully and prayerfully, blessing them and asking the deity to make a special dwelling place there. God might be everywhere, but some places are specially blessed with his presence, such as the human soul or the sacred images. Hindus pray before the deity to be seen – to make darshana. The deity sees them and they see the deity.

Every day the priest performs the arti ceremony. Arti uses light to worship the deity. The priest blows a conch shell at the beginning and end. He also rings a bell to attract the deity's attention and to call the worshippers.

He makes special offerings to the deity. These include incense, fire and water. The priest lights a lamp or candles on a tray. He moves the light around in a circle before the images. Then he passes it in front of the worshippers.

1. List the things the priest does during the day and put them in order.
2. Write at least four things that Hindus do which show that they believe the god is really present in the image in the temple.
3. a) Put in your own words the Hindus' reasons for worshipping light.
   b) Suggest your own reasons why light is important.

54

The temple, or mandir, is a meeting point between heaven and earth. It is a symbol of the universe, with carvings and images of the animal world, leading up to the human, and then the divine. These are shaped like mountains, because the gods live on high, in mystery and are the most powerful things. The central part of the temple is the 'womb', the place where the image of the god is kept. A tower goes up above this, representing the journey of the soul towards Moksha, liberation. The space in front of the shrine is covered and held up by pillars – this is the mandapa.

▲ *A Hindu temple at Khajuraho, India*

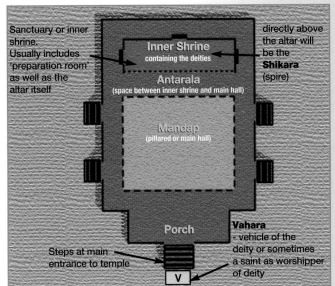

Sanctuary or inner shrine.
Usually includes 'preparation room' as well as the altar itself

Inner Shrine
containing the deities

directly above the altar will be the **Shikara** (spire)

Antarala
(space between inner shrine and main hall)

Mandap
(pillared or main hall)

Porch

Vahara
= vehicle of the deity or sometimes a saint as worshipper of deity

Steps at main entrance to temple

V

▲ *The layout of some Hindu temples*

55

1 **a)** Draw a plan of a Hindu temple and label each part.
  b) Put numbers on the plan to show which part you think
    (i) forms the boundary of the temple;
    (ii) contains the image of the temple's special god;
    (iii) is the place where shoes are left;
    (iv) contains another god or goddess;
    (v) is the symbol of a mountain.
2 **a)** Why are temples shaped like mountains?
  b) Talk about a time when you have climbed to the top of a mountain or a big hill. How has it felt, and did it give you a sense of greatness or power?
3 **a)** What do the carvings rising up on the outsides of the temples suggest?
  b) Draw your own carvings, showing animals, humans and then heaven or God.
  c) Talk, in groups, about how it feels to have something more powerful than humans. How might animals feel about us? If we mistreat animals, should we expect God to treat us fairly?

> ● 'Where women are respected, there lives God.'
> *The Laws of Manu*

Men and women are equally important in Hinduism. The Vedas tell Hindus to show more respect for their mother than for their father.

The mother is responsible for keeping the religious rituals in many Hindu families. She usually cares for the family shrine and performs puja. Often it is only the mother who keeps the rules about **fasting** at certain times.

Although the two sexes are equally important, Hindus nevertheless expect men and women to play different roles. Usually the men go out to work and the women are in charge of the home. In traditional Hindu families, the man gives his wages to his wife and she gives him any money he needs. The wife takes care of all the finances.

Despite this, a Hindu woman always depends on a man. In the Scriptures it says

> ● Father protects her in childhood, husband in youth, and sons in old age; a woman deserves to be looked after.

The last part means that a woman is too important to be left on her own. She must be looked after. In return, she should love her husband and be loyal and faithful to him.

Until the nineteenth century, it was usually only boys who went to school. Girls received an education within the home. They often learned about culture and the arts as well as cooking and housekeeping. Woman had a very traditional role in Indian society, as they did in all ancient societies. They also had an important role in passing down religious teachings, especially in stories.

Of course, there have always been some Hindu women who have behaved differently. They wrote books and fought in battle as well as being homemakers. Nowadays, however, all Hindu girls go to school and many have the opportunity to go to college or university and follow the same careers as men.

Traditionally, women have clearly defined roles within Hinduism. There is the ideal of the chaste, faithful wife. This might suggest a 'doormat' to Western ears, but is far from it in Hindu culture. The wife is very powerful within the home, and in the Mahabharata, the chaste wife Draupadi is **abused** before the assembled kings, and the warriors all die on the battlefield – such was their punishment. Draupadi was no meek and mild woman: she knocked down the warrior Jayadratha with one punch!

▲ *Jayadratha thought Draupadi was a meek and mild woman. How wrong he was!*

Hinduism teaches that if a chaste wife is insulted, the person who insults loses all their good karma.

Modern Hindu women seek more equality with men, and sometimes question the traditional roles. India had a woman Prime Minister, Indira Gandhi, in the twentieth century. Indian women have equal standing in the law, and equal voting rights.

Widows used to have a hard time, and some still do. Traditionally, a Hindu woman can marry only once, and if her husband dies when she is still young, she has to dress plainly and live with her husband's family. In the past, some high caste widows used to throw themselves onto their husband's funeral pyre. This custom was known as **sati**, from 'devoted wife'. The Hindu Scriptures declare that this ancient custom is not appropriate in the present age. Some Hindus say that the custom was originally voluntary. Later on, many widows were forced to meet such a death. Reformers **campaigned** against this, and it was outlawed in 1829.

▲ *Handprints that form a memorial to sati victims of the past*

The practice of giving a dowry is a common cause of concern in the Hindu world. The original system was that the parents would give gifts to their daughter at the time of her marriage. This was out of affection and so that she would feel comfortable in her new home. The parents would give whatever they could afford. In later years the system changed. The bride's parents were often expected to give a large dowry to the husband and his family at the time of the marriage. This was made illegal in 1961, but the custom is still widespread. Some poorer families despair if they have daughters but no sons, and there are terrible scandals in remoter parts of India, where baby girls are poisoned or abandoned.

Another problem can be when some families become greedy and demand more money after a marriage. If it is not given, they will arrange an 'accident' for the wife, who usually meets her death in a fire. The son is then free to remarry and collect another dowry!

Women have been campaigning since the nineteenth century to make significant changes in Hinduism, and many joined in the protests to end British rule in 1947. They hoped for changes when India was given independence. Some changes have taken place, but more needs to be done in their eyes to remove the bias towards sons in Hindu life.

In the past, women were not allowed to act as priests in temple worship, and on rarer occasions, they could not even attend. Some still cannot take part in initiation ceremonies (those who do so are not given the sacred thread out of respect for the difference between men's and women's bodies) or perform funeral rites for their parents. The bhakti movement included women in these activities and allowed them joyful access to God, through their praises, poems and songs.

▲ *Indira Gandhi (no relation to Mahatma) became India's first woman Prime Minister in 1966*

Hinduism has goddesses as well as gods. Those who believe that all the gods are aspects of Brahman see the goddesses as revealing feminine characteristics of God. Parvati, wife of Shiva, for example, represents the compassionate nature of God. Some goddesses show that women can be strong, determined and forceful.

The strangest figure for outsiders is Kali, a goddess of destruction and death. Hindus have representations of the darker side of life, remembering that new life often comes after suffering and loss.

▲ Krishna and his devotee, Radha

▲ Durga defeats the evil Mahisha

A number of Hindus consider Krishna to be the Supreme. His consort, and his beloved, is called Radha. She is the best devotee of Krishna. Still, in one sense, she can be seen as more powerful than Krishna, because her love always influences and controls him. Krishna's love of Radha represents the love of God for the universe. The universe praises God in return, and the devotee loves God.

When Mahisha the buffalo demon conquered the world and threatened to conquer heaven, Brahma, Shiva and Vishnu manifested their power in the form of a beautiful woman, Durga. She was a female deity who refused to marry, and was aggressive and assertive. She was given Shiva's armour, and a weapon from each of the deities. Durga fought Mahisha and killed him.

Durga has inspired women struggling for equal rights today. They take her as their example.

1 a) If you think of God as a woman, then what qualities come to mind?
b) Draw an image of God as Mother.
c) Why have some Hindu women used Durga as a role model? Do you think women are as strong willed and able as men?
2 a) What does Krishna and Radha's love for each other tell Hindus about God?
b) Design a film poster about a love story between God and humanity.

When Gandhi was **assassinated** in 1948, the Prime Minister of India, Jawaharlal Nehru, expressed the people's feelings when he said: *The light has gone out of our lives and there is darkness everywhere.*

- We will be non-violent; we will be truthful; we will not steal; we will not hoard; we will all wear **khadi** clothes; we will work with our hands; we will eat simple foods; we will treat people of all religions equally; and we will work for the [ending] of untouchability.

The huge crowd in the picture has gathered for a funeral in India. Some of those present have come from as far away as Britain. But most of them are Indian Hindus. Many of them believe that the dead man was a saint.

The man's name was Mohandas Gandhi, and he led the people of India towards **independence** from Britain in 1947. Many Indians call him Bapu or Father.

Gandhi was born in 1869. When he was just thirteen, his father arranged his marriage to a girl called Kasturbai. She was also thirteen so, at first, Kasturbai spent part of the time living with her parents, while Gandhi went back to school.

In 1888 Gandhi moved to England to study law. He left Kasturbai and his baby son behind. Friends in London asked him questions about Hinduism. Gandhi did not know all the answers, so he began to read the Bhagavad Gita. It became his favourite book.

Gandhi spent many years as a lawyer in South Africa. Indians were badly treated there. They could not travel first-class on trains. Only a few were allowed to vote. Gandhi led them in their fight for equality.

When the government announced that all Indians had to carry an identity card, Gandhi refused. So did many others. They were sent to prison. But they always protested in a peaceful way. Gandhi believed in ahimsa – non-violence towards any living thing. They campaigned for over twenty years before the South Africans ended the unjust laws against Indians.

Gandhi went home to India in 1915. He founded an ashram, a group of people who live according to religious ideals. The morning prayer meeting at the ashram always included these words:

▲ *Gandhi's funeral, 1948*

Gandhi did not agree with the rigid, hereditary caste system. He wanted the Untouchables to be able to go into temples and mix freely with other Hindus. Although Kasturbai did not agree with him at first, he took a family of Untouchables into his ashram. He gave them a new name. It was *Harijans*, which means *Children of God*.

In 1932, Gandhi began to fast as a protest against the treatment of Harijans. He was willing to die to show how strongly he felt. This is what he said a few hours after beginning his fast.

- I believe that if untouchability is really rooted out, it will **purge** Hinduism of a terrible blot. My fight against untouchability is a fight against the **impure** in humanity ... My fast is based in the cause of faith in the Hindu community, [and] faith in human nature itself. My cry will rise to the throne of the Almighty God.

Gandhi's fast *did* change some Hindus' minds. Harijans were allowed into temples. They could walk on any road and draw their water from any well. But not everybody was convinced. Life is still difficult for many Harijans. A Harijan woman, who went to live in Gandhi's ashram when she was a little girl, spoke many years later of her problems.

> ● I can't persuade my son to marry. He's confused about his caste. You see, my children's father was a Brahmin. Bapu arranged my marriage to him. But people here still hold it against my children that their mother was born a Harijan.

An example of non-violent protest was the salt march of 1930. Gandhi led a long march to the sea where the protesters made salt by boiling the sea water. This was a protest against a tax on salt that the British rulers of India had imposed. Many protesters were arrested.

Later, marchers set out for the salt factory and attempted to enter this and take it over, organising a huge 'sit in'. They were arrested or beaten up as they tried to enter, one by one. At no point did any of the protesters use violence. Their determination and moral courage led to a change in the law, and the Salt Acts were not applied as forcefully as before.

Gandhi believed that non-violence shamed the rulers, showing them to be unjust and bullies. Popular opinion was thus won by Gandhi, and international newspapers and radio stations also showed an interest in his moral struggle.

▲ *The Salt March, 1930*

He saw the strength of non-violence in **satyagraha**, 'the force of truth'. He believed that truth and right were on his side.

These sayings of Gandhi show the power he thought there was in non-violent protest:

> ● Non-violence is more powerful than all the armaments in the world.
>
> Non-violence is not passivity in any shape or form. It is the most active force in the world.
>
> In non-violence the masses have a weapon which enables a child, a woman, or even a decrepit old man to resist the mightiest government successfully.

60

1 For each of the words below, explain
  (i) what it means and
  (ii) how it is connected with Gandhi.
  independence; ashram; Bhagavad Gita; fasting; ahimsa.

2 **a)** What did Gandhi do to try to improve life for the Untouchables?
  b) Was he completely successful? Give reasons for your answer.

3 **a)** When a famous person dies, an article about him or her appears in newspapers. It is called an obituary. It usually includes only the good things about the person. Write an obituary of Gandhi.
  b) What things, if any, have you left out of Gandhi's obituary?

4 Do you think violence is wrong? Think of some ways of using non-violent protest today.

5 Imagine that you are a reporter for a foreign newspaper, watching the salt march. Describe what is happening, and why, and try to get your readers on Gandhi's side.

Everybody knows what it means if there's one of these signs outside a house.

▲ *Some Hindu families have moved to the UK*

The people who live there have sold their home and are moving to live somewhere else. Maybe their new house is in the same town or village. They will still see their friends. The children will still go to the same school. And the adults will stay in their jobs.

Perhaps they are going further away. So a new house also means new schools, jobs and friends. You may have experienced this, or know someone who has. Maybe someone in your class today is finding life a bit strange because they have recently moved.

Most people who move house stay in the same country. It is easier to be in a place where you speak the language and understand the **customs**. But sometimes people need to move to another country. Since the Second World War many Hindus have come to live in Britain. Some came from India in the 1950s because Britain invited people from the **Commonwealth nations** to help rebuild the country after the 1939–45 war. Often the father came on his own and then sent for his family when he had settled down.

However, most of the Hindus living in Britain came from countries in East Africa. Their ancestors had moved there to help the British by working on the railways in the late nineteenth century.

From the mid-1960s life was made very difficult for them by African **dictators** like Idi Amin of Uganda. They were forced to leave. Most Hindus chose to come to Britain.

Now there are about 500,000 Hindus in Britain. Sometimes they convert a hall or a room in a house into a temple. Some Hindu communities have built their own temples.

▲ *A Hindu temple in Leicester, England*

◄ *Indian teenagers wearing Western clothes*

Hindus have lived in Britain for many years now. Children have been born here, and they have grown up and had their own children. The present generation of Hindu teenagers tends to feel thoroughly British, following Western fashions in clothes and music. There can be a clash of cultures, though.

- Some parents are more traditional and young people, especially girls, may have to wear Indian style clothes at home.
- Hindu boys and girls might not be allowed to mix freely and go out with each other as their other friends do. Some parents might be very strict about keeping the sexes separate, or will insist that a boy and a girl have a companion with them to make sure they do not get tempted and go too far sexually.
- Some parents might want an arranged marriage, as is the custom in India. While the boy and girl can refuse a particular partner, they can feel pressurised. Some Hindu young people want to make their own choices, in the Western way.

Hindus might have to put up with racism. Having a different colour of skin, a different religion, or a way of dress, makes some people feel the need to call them names. A common insult is, 'You're taking our jobs!'. Remember that when the British government invited Hindus to come to this country, after the war, Britain needed all the help it could get. Many men had been killed in the war, cities and factories had been bombed and good, reliable workers were needed. In time, Hindu families created their own businesses and jobs.

A great number of Hindu teenagers have never been to India, and have lived in Britain all their life, as their parents might have done, too. Britain has always been made up of different races as a nation – the Scots, Irish, Saxons, Normans, Romans, for example. There is no such thing as a pure British race. A British person is someone who is born here, and who sees this as their homeland.

Hindus and other young Asians are merging Indian culture with British in many new ways, such as music. There are prominent Asian DJs who play at clubs and have mixes that blend Indian styles of music with Western. Western groups also take on Hindu influence, for example in some of Kula Shaker's songs. As the generations go on, there is a more self-confident, settled Asian presence in Britain.

1 Write a letter to an 'Agony Aunt' from a Hindu teenager. Choose some of the difficulties that he or she might face and write about these. What reply would the 'Agony Aunt' give?

2 Work out a role play where a person tries to answer a racist who says, 'Hindus only came to Britain to take our jobs!'

3 See if anyone in the class can bring in some examples of Asian mixes and play these. Compare these with tracks such as 'Govinda' by Kula Shaker. (Point out that 'Govinda' (cow-herder) is a name of Krishna.)

Glossary

abused – hurt, used wrongly

ancestors – relatives who lived before you

archaeologist – someone who finds out about life long ago

Aryans – tribes who invaded northern India about 3,500 years ago

assassinated – murdered

attain – reach

axis – the straight line about which the Earth turns

campaigned – tried to change something by persuading people

Commonwealth nations – countries that used to be part of the British Empire

conceived – begun to grow inside the mother

conch – large shell that is blown at the start of temple services

concoction – something mixed up

constellation – a group of stars

cremation – burning of a dead body

crematorium – where cremations take place

customs – habits which have lasted a long time

cycle – set of events which repeats itself

Dadaji – affectionate name for grandfather

Deity – god or goddess

devotees – people who worship a particular deity

dictator – ruler of country with complete power

discriminate – make a difference between

Equator – imaginary circle round the middle of the Earth

eternal – without beginning or end

fasting – going without food

grudge – dislike for a long time

henna – reddish-orange dye

Hindi – an Indian language

horoscope – diagram of the stars and planets

image – statue

impure – bad

independence – freedom from government by another country

influential – having an influence on people, someone who makes a difference

intermarry – become linked by marriage

ishta devata – chosen way

juggernaut – very large lorry

khadi – homespun cotton cloth

liberation – freedom

Madh – platform in middle of temple

mantra – word or phrase with special power

meditation – quiet thought

migrant – traveller, settling in another country

overwhelm – completely overcome

pardoned – forgiven

pining – longing for

prashad – blessed food, which is shared out among the worshippers

puja – personal act of worship of a deity at home

purge – make clean

pyre – pile of wood

Ramayana – poem which tells story of Rama

represent – stand for

residential – an area where people live

ritual – to do with religious occasion

sacred – holy

sacrifice – an offering to a God? or deity?

sadhu (holy man) – a wandering holy man and respected teacher

sage – wise person

sandalwood – sweet-smelling wood

sari – garment wrapped round the body

scantily – not enough to keep warm

shrine – holy place

Smritis – things which have been learned by heart

striving – working hard

sublime – perfect, beautiful, beyond words and time

symbol – something that stands for something else

techniques – ways of doing something

textiles – woven materials

traditions – customs handed down from parents to children

turmeric – powdered root used as dye

yoga – a discipline of body or mind

Index